THE
CHRISTIAN
PASTOR

THE
CHRISTIAN
PASTOR

■.■.■.■.■.■.■.■.■.■.■.■

WAYNE E. OATES

Assistant Professor of Psychology of Religion
Southern Baptist Theological Seminary

Philadelphia
THE WESTMINSTER PRESS

250V
Oa 8

116925

PRINTED IN THE UNITED STATES OF AMERICA

To My Wife and Son
Pauline and Bill

PREFACE

MANY are the tasks into which circumstances press the Christian pastor, but he thinks of himself at his best as being a shepherd of his flock, a minister of reconciliation whose task is the care and cure of souls in the face-to-face relationships with individuals. This book is intended to serve as a practical guide for the average pastor in a specific church as he " gives himself to this ministry."

Much that is valuable has been written on the important subject of the science of shepherding (as Washington Gladden called it, the " science of poimenics "). The claim that this book has to a hearing rests on its fivefold emphasis, some of which does not seem to be covered in the present literature. First, attention is given to the historical role and function of the pastor as a " man of crisis." Secondly, the theological context for Christian counseling and pastoral work, which in other places has been treated philosophically at best, is here interpreted in the light of the functional role of the pastor as a " symbolic " representative of God the Father, God the Son, God the Holy Spirit, and God at work in the world through the church. Thirdly, the Biblical concept of the work of a pastor, freed of most of the technical jargon drawn from the fields of psychiatry, psychology, and psychoanalysis, is emphasized here. Great truths have a tendency to be very old, and the Bible speaks in plainer language many of the truths to which scientific explorers have added fresh meaning by giving them a new name and a new use. The personal qualifications of a pastor, as set forth in the Bible, bring all the values of these new fields of research into focus.

Fourthly, the conditioning influences that ordinarily go unspoken

7

in most pastoral relationships are described in order that a pastor may be freed of a slavish dependence upon any one or two techniques through an appreciation of the social context in which he functions. And finally, the pastor who is actively engaged in the life of his church ordinarily is one who received his education at a time when courses and clinics in pastoral care and personal counseling had not yet been organized. He feels the need for guidance on the kind of literature to buy, to read, and to hand to persons who seek for specific help in literature. Therefore, definite suggestions are made all along the way in these pages as to the best literature in the whole field.

The title of this book, *The Christian Pastor,* was used in the late 1890's by Washington Gladden. The warm rays of the influence of this great pastor have given light and inspiration to me. However, I have sought to interpret this subject entirely afresh in the light of my generation's resources and needs. But I am indebted to him for his title.

I have been dependent upon others in writing these pages and my appreciation goes to many persons whom I could name. My students have been fellow explorers with me, and this book is an attempt to express my gratitude to them. Their difficult questions and unfailing loyalty have made this work possible. My teachers: W. R. Cullom, A. C. Reid, G. S. Dobbins, O. T. Binkley, Ralph Bonacker, Anton Boisen, J. B. Weatherspoon, and Harold W. Tribble have given me both information and inspiration as I have formulated these concepts. Professor Russell L. Dicks has been an experienced and encouraging guide in the step-by-step preparation of this manuscript. I am grateful for his counsel in the craft of authorship. My wife and son have made home a place of meditation and joyful companionship as I have worked.

Further, I cannot name, but only express my devoted reverence for, the many people who have sought my help as a counseling pastor. They have been my instructors in the ways of the human heart.

Wayne E. Oates

Louisville, Kentucky,
July 15, 1950.

CONTENTS

Part One

Part Two

Appendixes

9

PART ONE

THE PASTORAL TASK

CHAPTER I

THE CRISIS MINISTRY OF THE PASTOR

THE pastor moves from one crisis to another with those whom he shepherds. In a single day he may visit the mother of a new-born baby, give guidance to a person who is becoming a Christian, talk with a high school or college graduate about his lifework, unite a couple in marriage, comfort a person who is bereaved, call upon a person who is confronting a serious operation, and listen to the last words of a patient who is dying. Two thousand years of Christian ministry have conditioned Christians to expect their pastors at these times of crisis. Therefore, the Christian pastor comes to his task in the strength of a great heritage. Even though he feels a sense of awe in the presence of the mysterious and tremendous crises of life, he also feels a sense of security in the fact that his people both want and expect him to be present at their times of testing.

The crises of everyday living — birth, redemption, work, marriage, illness, bereavement, and death — are the shared experiences of all people in one way or another. They are the common ventures of life in which " the whole creation has been groaning in travail to-gether until now " (Rom. 8:22). The straitening anxieties of these times of crisis call for a reorganization of the total personality of an individual and his family, and the result may easily be disorgani-zation. These crises either strengthen or weaken an individual per-sonality; they are either-or situations which call for ethical choice, in-crease in emotional maturity, and additional spiritual resources. Therefore the careful and considerate attention of a skilled minister under the tutelage of the Holy Spirit in these crises often makes the difference between a spiritually mature and mentally healthy person and a spiritually retarded and mentally sick person.

Consequently, the minister is called upon, not necessarily to do " some new thing," but rather to do more scientifically and accurately the work that has been expected of him and to which he has been commissioned by the living Christ since the beginning of the Christian Era. In order to do this adequately in modern society, the pastor needs to take three practical steps: (1) He needs to plan his visitation and counseling in terms of these crises. (2) He needs to equip himself with the devotional literature of the Bible and Christian history concerning these crises. (3) He needs to know the psychological significance of these crises in the developmental history of a person.

The pastor who visits his people when they need him saves much lost motion in aimless and meaningless visitation. Visiting them in crises lends purpose and warmth, meaning and value to his call. Such calls establish a sense of rapport between him and his parishioners that serves as a foundation for all future pastoral care and personal counseling. The time that the pastor would otherwise spend in getting acquainted with people who ask for counseling help can be used for more meaningful purposes.

The equipment of Biblical and historical wisdom helps a pastor to deal with crises in his own life; with the " patience and comfort of the Scriptures " he has hope and can inspire hope in those to whom he ministers. The literature of the Bible and Christian history becomes pastoral aids in his hands, freeing him from hackneyed phrases and trite aphorisms that remind one of Job's comforters. Likewise, the simplicity of the psalms and other hymnbooks of the ages purifies the pastor's speech of technical theological and psychological jargon which has a minimum of emotional strength for the average person.

However, a pastor cannot afford to be untutored in the science of human nature and behavior. He needs also to recognize the psychological significance of these everyday crises in the developmental history of a person and a community. He can best learn this by studying the results of research on each of these crisis situations: birth, conversion, vocational choice, marriage, illness, bereavement, death. The bibliography at the end of this chapter lists some of the most helpful writings concerning these crises. Supervised clinical pastoral training in the care of persons most in need of help at such times is also a necessity. In these crises, a pastor can do much to

promote mental health and to prevent mental disease if he has taken
the time to learn the difference between mental health and mental
disease. If he has not so equipped himself, he may even do much to
cause mental disease by unwittingly misunderstanding the dynamics
of personality formation and disintegration.

Therefore, both a thorough knowledge of the Bible and Christian
history and an empirical knowledge of the psychology of these crises
are essential. But a " focused perspective " of the two is even more important. The art of living amid the everyday crises of normal growth
is the province of common concern for both the pastor and the medical psychologist. In the reactions of people to these crises, the interests of religion and medical psychology intersect, both to meet and
to part, in the mutually necessary emphases which they sponsor. In
deed and in fact, when the religious and psychological points of
view are focused upon each of these crises, the pastor gets a true-to-
life, " polaroid " perspective that has both the breadth of empirical
research and the depth of religious experience and values. Such a perspective of the crises of birth, conversion, the choice of a vocation,
marriage, illness, bereavement, and death may be discussed sugges-
tively here.

A. The birth of a child in a home is a crisis experience in which
the pastors of all communions are expected to take an interest. This
may be an occasion of great happiness and good fortune, or it can
be one of tragedy and grief. At the very best, the birth of a child
necessitates a total reorganization of routine in the home and brings
about subtle changes in relationships between the members of the
family. If the husband has been mothered by the wife, he now is dis-
placed by one who really needs mothering. If the wife has been ac-
customed to going anywhere she pleases without regard to the needs
of her husband, she now is tied down to the needs of the child. If
there is another child in the home, the coming of this child means
that the attention of the parents must be shared between the two
children. From an economic point of view, the child increases the
responsibility of the parents considerably and calls for a shift in
their personal values. From a psychological point of view, the par-

ents' concepts of themselves change perceptibly and they find it difficult to imagine what they were like before they had children. Therefore, parenthood may be either a cohesive or a disjunctive crisis in
the life of an individual and a family.

The churches have always laid great store by the importance of
children, and the Jewish and the Christian religions are as unique
in their evaluation of children as they are in their concepts of God.
As Luke describes the ministry of John the Baptist, the function of
the prophetic religions has been " to turn the hearts of the fathers
to the children " (Luke 1:17). Likewise, it may be said that the
birth of a child has a way of turning the minds of some parents to a
worshipful consideration of their own relationship to God. In other
instances, the parents may become so emotionally involved with the
child that they lose interest in everyone else. It is not unusual at all
for a young couple to use the advent of a child as a reason for in-
difference to the church and other community activities. Such a
family becomes ingrown upon itself and the children themselves become objects of worship and in turn are expected to worship the
parents.

Group instruction in family life education and individual pastoral
attention can do much toward laying the foundation for a well-
balanced parent-child relationship through the years. Quite often a
pastor is asked for specific information on child care and the emotional problems of children. Through close co-operation with his
state board of health, the minister can have dependable insights and
good literature to aid him in his pastoral care of young families. Pastoral visitation in the home and hospital, coupled with brief worship
services of gratitude and dedication for parents and children, will be
valuable for pastors in nonliturgical communions. In those communions where christening and baptism are used in this ministry, the
pastor will do well to lay hold of these significant occasions as opportunities to encourage the proper relationship between the child
and his parents.

B. Religious conversion is a crisis in which the pastor serves as a
minister of reconciliation, not between a child and his parents, but

between an adult and the God and Father of our Lord Jesus Christ. Not all conversion experiences meet this definition; therefore, not all of them are constructive changes in personality. Rather, many of them are not changes at all but mere perpetuations in different garb of the same infantile character. In these cases, the conversion or pseudo conversion is an abortive, disintegrative miscarriage of creativity. It becomes a thorn in the flesh that cannot be assimilated into the rest of the personality, continuing as if it were entirely apart from the rest of the self. Such a projection of religious concepts into the mind, of religious practices into the habits, of religious values into the conscience, and of religious feelings into the affective depths of the personality increases the unhappiness and the lack of unity in the person. As one person has said, "My misery began when I was baptized."

But on the other hand, the fact remains that for many persons the conversion experience is the beginning of their true selfhood. They achieve spiritual autonomy by "getting their own religion" apart from that of their parents which has been breathed for them in their mothers' lullabies. Their conversion points them into the direction of a happy vocational and marital choice and becomes that portion of their personality which arises at the very core of life. In a homely metaphor, this type of conversion experience becomes the stack pole around which the rest of the personality is organized. Allport has well described it by saying that such religious experience is a man's "audacious bid . . . to bind himself to creation and to the Creator . . . his ultimate attempt to enlarge and to complete his own personality by finding the supreme context in which he rightly belongs." [1]

Probably the main determinant between these two kinds of conversion in any given case is the kind of spiritual relationship that existed between the person who is converted and his parents. Historically and psychologically the parents have always been the first pastors and priests of the individual. But next to the parents' determinative influence is the kind of pastoral care the individual receives from the minister of his church. The chaplains of state hospitals can tell

[1] Gordon W. Allport, *The Individual and His Religion*, p. 142.

the pastor a good deal about the part that pastoral neglect and mal-practice can play in aggravating rather than healing mental disease at the crisis of conversion. No single factor is more determinative in quickening and strengthening personality growth and health than is the conversion experience that goes to the depths of the emotional life of a person. Wise pastoral care often makes the difference be-tween an abortive and a creative conversion experience.

C. The completion of education and the choice of a full-time vo-cation is another crisis common to all persons who participate in life to the fullest. Here again the person who feels a sense of responsi-bility to God for his life naturally turns to the minister for vocational guidance. This becomes the door into the confidence of young people which the pastor can most easily enter. High school and college stu-dents may be defensive about their religious loyalties and resistive about their love lives, but they are eager to talk with a genuinely interested person about what they are going to do with their lives.

Here the pastor confronts the strains and pressures of our com-petitive society upon growing personalities. When a person has com-pleted his education, he is on his own. He is expected to prove him-self, to make something out of himself, to get up in the world, to do as well as the rest of his classmates, and to be above those of his own age. This is closely geared in with his marital hopes, and quite often the person becomes stalemated when his marital hopes and his vocational objectives conflict with each other.

Here again the person is in an either-or situation: He may be comfortable with a vocational objective that is in keeping with his abilities, or he may have received such impossible goals for himself that he thinks of himself as nothing in comparison with them. He may enjoy a reasonable amount of competition, or he may be so overwhelmed by any amount of competition that he prefers to get drunk rather than take a chance on failing in his work. He may have ability to accept his own failures, or he may be so afraid of failure that he cannot act at all. He may have a creative imagination and an active foresight, but he may prefer dreaming *about* his goals to walking *toward* them. At any rate, the completion of education and the choice of a full-time job is a major crisis.

The pastor can do much toward preparing the youth of his church for this crisis through group education in vocational opportunities and responsibilities. His personal interest and firm confidence in people quite frequently serves to cushion the crisis and to guide them through discouragement and anxiety. The practical help a pastor can offer high school and college graduates in his church in finding happy places of work will be time well afforded. Some pastors find the whole months of May and June dominated with the needs of their young people in this sphere. If the pastor can plan with the whole church on ways and means of helping the young people through this crisis, the problems in religious skepticism, juvenile delinquency, and other forms of adolescent rebellion can be reduced considerably.

D. Marriage is a crisis in the lives of the people who take it seriously enough to consult a minister. Traditionally marriage has been the concern of the churches, and even in the secular culture of today those who marry turn to pastors for religious sanction of the step they are taking. Marriage is a crisis, not only for the persons who are marrying, but also for their parents and siblings. For this cause both the man and the woman leave their fathers and mothers, precipitating a radical reorganization of life both in their own lives and in the lives of the families from which they come. It seems almost ironical, but the family by its very nature was established with the ultimate biological and spiritual objective of being dissolved in order that new families might be formed.

Therefore, all the early family relationships and parental training in religion are brought into focus at the time of marriage. The concept of the self of an individual undergoes marked changes. The routines of living of marital partners are transformed as they shift the centers of their attention from themselves to each other. Marriage brings religious values into bolder relief, and shows up the presence or absence of emotional stability with a fluoroscopic accuracy.

The minister may or may not function as a marriage and family counselor when young persons confer with him about wedding cere-monies. This depends upon his willingness to take the time to do so and his discipline of himself in the careful study of the principles and techniques of marriage and family counseling. When the pastor does this faithfully, he often makes the difference between a success-ful marriage and a failure, and in other instances he can make the difference between an unhappy marriage and a happy marriage. The pastor who does not attempt to give family life education on a group level and marriage and family counseling on an individual level, however, has no right to preach against divorce. His own pastoral neglect may be directly responsible for the " hardness of heart " that made the writ of divorcement possible and even necessary.

E. Physical illness sooner or later becomes a crisis in most people's lives unless they die sudden or violent deaths. The physically ill person loses his independence and must lean on other people in a relative state of helplessness. He is shocked by the abruptness of pain, panicked by the thought of sustained helplessness or death, and con-fused by the opinions and procedures of the medical experts in whose hands rests his life. He may become isolated by his illness to a life of self-concern, and his mind searches in its loneliness for some ex-planation of the mystery of his suffering. He confronts the alternative of dealing constructively with these problems, or of adopting his illness as a chronic way of life. Here again is an either-or situation in which the individual and his family need the help of a skilled min-ister as they pass through the different stages of an illness.

The research of psychosomatically oriented physicians has estab-lished the fact that emotional tension and deeply rooted anxieties may cause, aggravate, or prolong an illness. Likewise, physical ill-ness, even the sort requiring surgery, is often the prelude to psychotic disturbances.

The minister is expected to be a visitor of the sick, and the healing ministry is a part of the threefold commission of Jesus — preaching, teaching, and healing. The Reformation marked the recovery of the preaching ministry from sacramentalism; the translation of the Bible into the vernacular marked the recovery of the teaching ministry

from the monastery; now the development of clinical pastoral training and the closer co-operation of medicine and the ministry gives
promise to recover the healing ministry from the magic and super-
stition of relic worship and primitive faith healing cults.

Many ministers look upon the visitation of the sick as a chore,
dreading the discomfort of being around people who are helpless and
in pain. But the minister who takes seriously the importance of
physical and mental illnesses as spiritual crises of major proportions
will find an effectual door of service and instruction set before him.
He will become an original explorer into the laws of character that
work themselves out before his eyes. He will be doing genuine
laboratory work in the patient study of the facts of human nature.
As Washington Gladden says: " The people with whom he is dealing will know [that] he is speaking from observation [and not]
tradition; he must be able to say: ' We speak that we do know, and
testify that we have seen.' " [2]

F. Bereavement is another crisis in the life of every person who
takes the risk of loving someone other than himself. The course of
normal grief extends over a more lengthy period of time than is
ordinarily assumed. It moves through stages of shock; numbness of
feeling which seems to have organic involvements as well as psychic
ones; a refusal to accept the reality of the death of the loved one; a
period of semiconscious fantasy along with a selective memory of
events that happened in relation to the loved one; a gradual return
of feeling and a flood of grief; and a transference of feelings to a
new object of affection.

The Christian community has intuitively provided ways and means
of ministering to bereaved persons, and the pastor can depend upon
the help of his congregation at times like this in the care of bereaved
persons. Unusually powerful guilt feelings are quite often at work
in bereavement, and subtle deifications of the dead loved one can
cause the bereaved person to become mentally ill.

The pastor is the only trained person into whose hands the care
of the bereaved is wholly committed at the time of the crisis. He has

[2] *The Christian Pastor and the Working Church,* p. 94.

no competition here from other professions. His message of immortality and the transcendence of the eternal over the temporal is the only " renewal " of the mind of the grief-stricken that can transform them. The pastor becomes a traveler between life and death with his parishioners at these times, guiding them through the valley of the shadow of death. He cannot leave this ministry to professional mourners and morticians. He has been appointed " to comfort all that mourn; . . . to give unto them a garland for ashes, the oil of joy for mourning, the garment of praise for the spirit of heaviness; that they may be called trees of righteousness, the planting of the Lord, that he may be glorified " (Isa. 61:2, 3).

G. Death is a crisis that does not exempt anyone. The ministry to the dying, as they are surrounded by their family, is inseparable from the ministry to the bereaved. It, however, is one of the most intensely personal and individualized services that a pastor renders. The dying person's request for the pastor's time and attention takes precedence over all others, and the pastor should feel deep gratitude for the honor of being sent for at this final crisis of a person's life.

The minister needs to recognize the fact that many persons may be said to die mentally before they do physically. The presence of heart action and respiration are not indications of the presence of mind. The weight of sedation, the weariness of the struggle with pain, and the presence of infection in the organism militate against rationality in a dying person.

Furthermore, the person who is aware of impending death is quite often more concerned about his loved ones than about himself. Barriers that exist between him and those whose approval he considers most worth-while are problems to him. He is anxious about what will happen to them when he is gone, especially if some of them are small children.

Quite regularly the pastor is called upon to listen to the confession of the secret sins of dying persons, because they are concerned with middle walls of partition that separate them from God. The need for confessional ministry, although not formalized, remains an abiding reality in the spiritual hunger of the dying. Here, also, the pastor shares in the radiant pilgrimage which triumphant Christians make from mortality into immortality. To him are granted glimpses into eternity in spite of his childlike blunders in the use of God's instruments of redemption.

From birth to death and at every significant point between, the Christian pastor is commissioned by Christ and expected by his community to bring the mind of Christ and the reality of the Holy Spirit to bear upon the crises that people face. Several crises have been described here. Others, less universally confronted, but nevertheless acutely meaningful to those who do experience them, could be named. Social crises of war, famine, flood, and fire assail people en masse. Divorce and mental illness are crises of family and personal disorganization that are increasing in prevalence.

The pastor, along with all others engaged in humanitarian tasks, is a man of crisis for such times as these. Having inherited such a ministry, he can conserve his birthright and add to it his own personal spiritual fortune by assimilating all that modern research has to offer him in discipline and technique and by understanding Biblical truth in terms of human needs. Thus he "brings out of his treasure what is new and what is old" (Matt. 13:52).

SUGGESTED READINGS

The following bibliography is suggestive of the empirical research and practical guidance by authoritative scientists on the common crises of life:

A. Birth

1. Otto Rank, *The Trauma of Birth.* Harcourt, Brace and Company, 1929.
2. Sigmund Freud, *The Problem of Anxiety.* W. W. Norton & Company, Inc., 1936.
3. Pamphlet publications that can be used in individual counseling and family life education groups:

    How Does Your Baby Grow? Maternity Center Association.

    Prenatal Care. Federal Security Agency, Social Security Administration, U.S. Children's Bureau.

    Making the Grade as Dad, by Walter and Edith Neisser. Public Affairs Pamphlet No. 157.

    What Makes a Good Home? Child Study Association of America.

What Makes Good Habits — The Beginnings of Discipline. Child Study Association of America.

Are We Helping or Hindering Our Children?, by George S. Stevenson. The National Committee for Mental Hygiene, Inc.

Enjoy Your Child — Ages 1, 2, and 3, by James L. Hymes, Jr. Public Affairs Pamphlet No. 141.

Some Special Problems of Children Aged 2 to 5 Years, by Nina Ridenour and Isabel Johnson. The National Mental Health Foundation, Inc.

Your Child from One to Six. Federal Security Agency, Social Security Administration, U.S. Children's Bureau, Publication 30.

Understand Your Child — from 6 to 12, by Clara Lambert. Public Affairs Pamphlet No. 144.

B. Conversion

1. Anton T. Boisen, *The Exploration of the Inner World.* Willett, Clark & Company, 1936.
2. William James, *Varieties of Religious Experience.* Modern Library, Inc., 1901.
3. A. D. Nock, *Conversion.* The Clarendon Press, 1933.
4. G. W. Allport, *The Individual and His Religion.* The Macmillan Company, 1950.

C. Vocational Guidance

1. *The American Council on Education Studies.* Series VI — Student Personnel Work, Nos. 1 to 4. 744 Jackson Place, Washington, D.C.
   No. 1. *Educational Counseling of College Students,* Bragdan, Brumbaugh, Pillard, and Williamson.
   No. 2. *Occupational Orientation of College Students,* Cowley, Hoppock, Williamson.
   No. 3. *Social Competence and College Students,* Jones.
   No. 4. *Religious Counseling of College Students,* Merriam.
2. Public Affairs Pamphlet, *What It Takes to Make Good in College,* by Samuel L. Hamilton.
3. J. Oliver Nelson, *We Have This Ministry: Church Vocations for Men and Women.* Association Press, 1946.
4. Alexander Miller, *Christian Faith and My Job.* Association Press, 1946.

D. Marriage

1. William Lyon Phelps, *Marriage.* E. P. Dutton & Co., Inc., 1941.
2. Ernest and Catharine Groves, *Dynamic Mental Hygiene, with Special Emphasis on Family Counseling.* Stackpole Sons, 1946.
3. Sidney E. Goldstein, *Marriage and Family Counseling; A Manual for Ministers, Doctors, Lawyers, Teachers, Social Workers and*

Others Engaged in Counseling Service. McGraw-Hill Book Company, Inc., 1945.

4. Morris Fishbein and E. W. Burgess, *Successful Marriage.* Doubleday & Company, Inc., 1947.

5. Ernest R. Groves, *The Family and Its Social Functions.* J. B. Lippincott Company, 1940.

6. F. W. Brink, *This Man and This Woman; A Guide for Those Contemplating Marriage.* Association Press, 1948.

E. Illness

1. Richard L. Cabot and Russell L. Dicks, *The Art of Ministering to the Sick.* The Macmillan Company, 1936.

2. Carroll A. Wise, *Religion in Illness and Health.* Harper & Brothers, publishers, 1942.

3. Seward Hiltner, *Religion and Health.* The Macmillan Company, 1943.

4. Helen F. Dunbar, *Mind and Body: Psychosomatic Medicine.* Random House, Inc., 1947.

5. Edward Weiss and O. S. English, *Psychosomatic Medicine.* W. B. Saunders Company, 1943.

6. Russell L. Dicks, *My Faith Looks Up.* The Westminster Press, 1949.

F. Bereavement

1. E. Lindemann, " Symptomatology and Management of Acute Grief," *American Journal of Psychiatry,* 101:141–148, 1944.

2. J. L. Liebmann, *Peace of Mind,* Chapter VI, " Grief's Slow Wisdom." Simon and Schuster, Inc., 1946.

3. J. L. Liebmann, *et al., Psychiatry and Religion,* Chapter Ten, " The Grief Situation." The Beacon Press, Inc., 1948.

4. W. F. Rogers, *Ye Shall Be Comforted.* The Westminster Press, 1950.

G. Death

1. Leo Tolstoi, *The Death of Ivan Ilyich.*

2. D. Elton Trueblood, *The Common Ventures of Life.* Harper & Brothers, publishers, 1949.

3. Russell L. Dicks, *Pastoral Work and Personal Counseling,* Revised Edition. The Macmillan Company, 1949.

Chapter II

THE SYMBOLIC ROLE OF THE PASTOR

The Christian pastor enters the responsibilities of his crisis ministry in the strength of the oldest calling among men. His role and function as a minister have been, through centuries of Christian culture, bred into the deeper levels of the consciousness of those whom he serves. Therefore, he has symbolic as well as personal influence, and the symbolic power of his role gives him a strength far beyond that of his own personal appeal to people. Paul described it well when he said, " We are ambassadors for Christ, God making his appeal through us " (II Cor. 5:20). The pastor represents and symbolizes far more than himself. He represents God the Father, he serves as a reminder of Jesus, he is an instrument of the Holy Spirit, and he is the emissary of a specific church.

This fact elevates the importance of the unique structure and function of a pastor's interpersonal relationships with people. It places in proper perspective the specific techniques of pastoral care and personal counseling and reveals the inadequacy of stereotyped advice in given situations. The careful, intelligent, and devoted management of the unique interpersonal relationship of a pastor to an individual or group becomes the normative definition of pastoral care and personal counseling. As such, the pastoral task is the participation in the " divine-human encounter."

All this implies a Christian context of basic theological axioms for pastoral care and personal counseling. The sovereignty of God, the principle of incarnation whereby the Word was made flesh, the activity of the Holy Spirit in contemporary living, and the function of the Church as the Body of Christ — these are the realities which the pastor symbolizes and represents. In pastoral care and personal counseling they become functional realities rather than theoretical topics of discussion. The analysis, therefore, of the symbolic role of the pastor provides an interpretation of his relationship to people in terms of his relationship to God. Such an approach gives *a theological framework for pastoral care and personal counseling*. Such a framework is needed lest the strength of secular concepts of counseling and psychotherapy force the pastor into a role and a relationship that are foreign to his unique place in society and in history.

I. THE PASTOR AS A REPRESENTATIVE OF GOD

" God making his appeal through us." — II Cor. 5:20.

Late one evening a minister received a call to come to a ward in the local hospital. Upon arrival he found an elderly farmer who had just been admitted. The man looked frightened and lonely, but a natural sense of humor welled up from beneath his anxiety. The minister introduced himself, and the patient said: " I heard that you would come if I asked for you. It's mighty kind of you, because I need you. You have heard that story in the Bible about how some fellows was cutting wood one day and the ax flew off the handle and fell in the river. They had to call the man of God to help them get it out. Well, I sure have had the ax to fly off the handle with me. I never been sick a day in my life, and all of a sudden things went wrong and they told me that I have cancer of the colon. I got to be cut on Monday morning. The ax has come off the handle with me, and when the nurse told me that a man of God was close by, I sent straightway for you to help me get the ax out of the creek."

People like this man still search out Christian pastors when they need friendship, encouragement, guidance, reconciliation, and relief from guilt. They seek their pastor because he is the man of God; he symbolizes the presence of God as a loving Father and as the center of all moral rightness. People of every condition turn to the minister because he represents the universal gospel of the eternal God. This universality means something more than geographical inclusiveness; it also means that *all* manner of people come to the Christian minister with *all* manner of problems. The Christian pastor, therefore, cannot select his clientele; he cannot eliminate those whose plight does not come under the classification of his specialty; neither can he pass hopeless cases to someone else. Regardless of the other ministers to humanity who may be serving his people (whether those servants be doctors, nurses, lawyers, social workers, psychiatrists, welfare workers, or public-school teachers), the pastor, by virtue of his role as a man of God, can never consider his people as being some other person's responsibility to the exclusion of his own. *He cannot pass his ministry to anyone else.* This is the distinctive difference between the Christian pastor as a servant of men and other people who are also engaged in humanitarian helpfulness.

The Christian pastor, then, is a representative of God, commissioned to bring the ruling sense of the presence of God to bear upon the conflict-weary lives of men and women. He is an apostle of redemption and reconciliation, a practicer of the art of communion with God. As such the pastor is concerned with the salvation of the *whole* personalities of his people through an effective relationship to God in Christ, rather than with the readjustment of this or that part of their lives.

As a representative of God, the minister is a reminder of all the parental training in the ways of right doing that his people received in childhood. These precepts, regardless of their truth or error, have become incorporated parts of their psychic lives. Consequently, the minister may find persons reacting to him in much the same way they did to their parents, and equating the precepts of their parents with the wisdom of God. The minister confronts the task of disentangling the good gifts of parents to their children from the much more excellent gifts of the Heavenly Father that are available through a personal experience of the Holy Spirit. Thus religious experience becomes firsthand and intimately personal rather than traditional and customary.

Again, the minister as a representative of God becomes a visible embodiment of *conscience*. Therefore, many will draw the fig leaves of respectability over the naked places of their souls lest their minister come to know them as they really are. By its very nature, the role of the minister is a judgmental role, and he cannot avoid the fact that a moralistic connotation is placed upon his presence. Every pastor, therefore, needs to avoid the error of thinking that the persons with whom he counsels appear in the same spiritual clothing to him that they do to those to whom they are more closely related. The minister's task is to discover the real selves of his people and to be the kind of minister with whom they can associate without pretension. At the same time, suffice it to say, the quiet dignity of a minister's own presence is often more of a rebuke to his people than any verbal censure he could pour upon them.

The strange power of a judgmental presence reminds the Christian pastor of his ever-present temptation to *supplant* rather than to represent God. A minister may easily be lured into substituting his own sovereignty for that of God, " in order that the excellency may be of himself rather than of God." The matchless insights of Hawthorne in his *Scarlet Letter,* and Maugham in his *Rain* are subtle reminders that the minister too is human and not divine. His relative degree of authority is derived by reason of the One whom he symbolizes; therefore, his greatest temptation is to assume that it originated with himself, to confuse the symbolism of his role with the reality of God.

Within the personality of every individual who turns to the pastor for help is the active tendency to make a god out of the minister, with an unconscious need to idolize and desecrate him at the same time. This has been called the " unreal need for a god in human form." [3] One way the minister may give in to this idolatrous demand is to require strict conformity to his will and ideas which he gives to his people in the form of advice. A very common daydream of ministers is that of seeing their people do just as they want them to do, seeing their own wills incarnated in the lives of their people. As Oscar Wilde describes this feeling, " There is something enthralling in projecting one's soul into someone's else gracious form, and letting it tarry there for a moment, to hear one's own intellectual views echoed back; to convey one's temperament into another as though it were some strange and subtle perfume." [4]

Another way a minister may substitute his relative authority for

[3] Otto Rank, *Will Therapy, and Truth and Reality,* p. 63. Alfred A. Knopf, 1945.
[4] *The Picture of Dorian Gray,* p. 38. The World Publishing Company, 1942.

the sovereignty of God in the lives of his people is to use them as means for his own chosen ends rather than treating them as ends in themselves by reason of the fact that they are sacred human personalities " for whom Christ died." Thus the pastor may let his function as an administrator, a builder of an organization, a promoter of a budget, or the leader of a crusade come into conflict with his representation of God. He must become a god himself in order that he may manipulate his people toward his own predestined goal.

Also, a minister may yield to pressure and make his people's decisions for them; in doing so, he, like Jiminy Cricket, becomes their official conscience for them. He takes responsibility away from them, which means that he takes their freedom from them and enslaves himself with them. The minister's task is to co-operate in the growth of human personalities that have been born of God. An individual does not become a person in his own right until he has exercised his own free powers of decision, and accepted the responsibility for the consequences of his decisions. As the Christian pastor stands in the holy of holies of men's souls, they may say to him, " You tell me what to do, and then I know it will be right." If the pastor gently but firmly moves this responsibility back to them and increases their confidence in their own ability to find the way of God, later he may have them come back and say to him, " All my life I have had people tell me what to do, and when they did, it seemed that almost against my own will I found myself doing just the opposite from the advice they gave me."

Something strong in human personality reaches out for an idol, but something eternal in human personality that outlasts both the idol and the desire for the idol says, " Cast down imaginations and everything that exalts itself against the knowledge of God." The unreal need for a god in human form clutches at the minister's desire to supplant God, but if he yields himself to this need, he in turn becomes an idol cast down when those whom he exploits discover that he also is human.

Therefore, the Christian pastor's objective is to free persons from bondage to their own self-reflections in the mirrors of their chosen idols and to bring them into a life-giving loyalty to Christ. In this drastic cutting of affectionate bonds, they are likely to shift their idolatry to the pastor, saying as did the people at Lystra and Derbe, " The gods have come down to us in the likeness of men! " All the while they may still be sitting on their own household gods just in case they are wrong. Thus the sovereignty of God becomes a continuously thrown-down gauntlet before the minister. If he lets it go unchallenged and accepts the dependent worship of the person, the last state is worse than the one before. If the minister accepts the challenge and refuses the prerogatives of God, then he faces a struggle with his own childish desires for omnipotence.

To symbolize the reality of God, therefore, calls for a unique kind of dedication. The Christian pastor knows that he has the treasure of this ministry in an earthen vessel. Insight into the earthenness of his own humanity prompts him to confess that the excellency of the power is of God and not himself. David E. Roberts clarifies the issues confronting the pastor when he says:

" The danger of ' playing God ' in the lives of people, which certainly must not be minimized, should not blind us to the facts that men can be instruments in the service of healing power. The endowments and skills of an individual are immeasurably enhanced by the fact that he is the symbol of something much greater than himself — namely, the drive toward fellowship, wholeness and honesty which is deeply rooted in human life." [5]

The security of the pastor arises out of his dependence upon the Chief Shepherd rather than from the completeness of his knowledge, the power of his own personality, or the cleverness of his techniques of dealing with people. He finds guidance for his pastoral practice in the Chief Shepherd, " who, though he was in the form of God, did not count equality with God a thing to be grasped, but emptied himself, taking the form of a servant, being born in the likeness of men. And being found in human form he humbled himself and became obedient unto death, even death on a cross " (Phil. 2:6–8).

Just such a renunciation lies at the base of all effective representa-

[5] *Psychotherapy and a Christian View of Man,* p. 53. Charles Scribner's Sons, 1950.

tion of God. Paul describes it best when he says, " We have renounced disgraceful, underhanded ways; we refuse to practice cunning or to tamper with God's word, but by the open statement of the truth we would commend ourselves to every man's conscience in the sight of God " (II Cor. 4:2).

II. The Pastor as a Reminder of Jesus

" God . . . has shone in our hearts to give the light of the knowledge of . . . God in the face of Christ." — II Cor. 4:6.

The pastor is related to people " as though it were in Christ's own stead." It is his personal motive to have in himself the mind that was in Christ Jesus. The request of the Greeks when they said, " We wish to see Jesus," is the unspoken need of those to whom the Christian pastor ministers. He symbolizes and reminds them of Jesus.

Therefore, the central objective of all *pastoral* care and personal counseling is that " Christ be formed " in the personality of the individuals who seek help.

Therefore, the principle of incarnation in continued action requires that the Christian pastor be a man of faith, " working through love." Hereby the minister becomes a permissive shepherd who loves his sheep rather than a pseudo sovereign who rules his subjects. The pastoral task is a voluntary relationship of shared affection.

Because of this affectionate tie of personal good will and loving identification, people can trust the motives of the minister and confide in him at times when they would be suspicious of their own family, their employer, or their physician. This may be called " the relationship of a trusted motive," whereby the pastor, by reason of the infinite love which he symbolizes, is given access to the holy of holies of men's confidence. This is an indispensable necessity in the relationship of a pastor to anyone whom he helps.

Therefore, the Christian shepherd must be continually at the business of examining his own motives for his face-to-face ministry to his people. He cannot hide tawdry motives of financial greed, love for domination, or erotic concern from those to whom he seeks to minister. The demons of fear, suspicion, greed, hatred, and exploitation know their own kind before they see them coming. Unconscious needs meet unconscious resistances, and nothing is hidden that is not revealed in the intimacy of the pastoral situation. A relationship of a trusted motive prevails only when a Christian pastor voluntarily accepts and effectively carries through with his role as a representative of the love of Christ. He is a servant of men for Jesus' sake. The effectiveness of all pastoral procedures depends upon the singleness of this motivation, and the ineffective use of the best techniques of counseling can be explained by the adulteration of this motive.

Other names have been given to this relationship of a trusted motive by explorers in the field of pastoral care and personal counseling. Rollo May calls it "empathy," whereby the pastor "feels his way into" the life situation of the person who seeks his help. Russell Dicks, in his earlier works, called it "rapport," by which he means a positive emotion of "good will, confidence, trust, affection, and its deeper sense . . . love." [6] R. H. Edwards, in his book *A Person-minded Ministry,* describes it as a "sense of togetherness" which exists between two people because they share confidence in mutual values, goals, and loyalties. However it is named, this relationship of a trusted motive is actually the power of "faith working through love" to heal humanity's hurt, to cast out fear, and to break down middle walls of partition that separate helpless people from sources of divine strength.

The psychological fact under consideration here is called "identification." This is the process whereby one person takes into himself the character traits of another because of his confidence in him, his love for him, and his desire to be like him. The law of identification on the divine-human level and in terms of religious psychology is known as worship. Personality takes the form of the object of its adoration; therefore, it is formed and transformed through the power of love.

The earliest illustrations of this power are found in the parent-child relationship, whereby the character of a child is formed into a

---

[6] *Marriage and Family Living,* Vol. III, No. 4, "Current Trends in Counseling: A Symposium."

positive likeness or a negative reaction formation of the actual character of his parents. The character formations of children are largely the result of the personal behavior patterns of their parents and are only remotely related to the moral preachments and oral instructions of their parents. As the wisdom of Whitman suggests:

" There was a child went forth every day,
  And the first object he look'd upon, that object he became,
  And that object became part of him for the day or a certain part of the day,
  Or for many years or stretching cycles of years. . . .
  His own parents, he that had father'd him and she that conceived him in her womb and birthed him,
  They gave this child more of themselves than that,
  They gave him afterward every day — *they and of them became part of him* . . .
  These became part of that child who went forth every day, and who now goes, and will always go forth every day." [7]

The process of identification works in the pastoral relationship to groups and to individuals in much the same way that it does in the parent-child relationship. The Word becomes flesh through the power of faith working through love; in so far as the minister participates in the mind of Christ toward people, the pastoral relationship becomes the transmission line of the character of Christ. Therefore, the able minister of the new covenant of the love of Christ does not look upon his work as the scribes did, i.e., orally transmitting a literal law that is to be carried out legally to the last iota, but as the effective manifestation of the Spirit of Christ. He is a minister, " not in a written code but in the Spirit; for the written code kills, but the Spirit gives life " (II Cor. 3:6).

The pastor is confronted with the practical task of finding out what is bothering the persons who come to him. He must first be a student of the person in the privacy of his own mind before he can be a teacher of the person in the interpretation of his difficulties. Also, the minister must have a certain amount of knowledge of ways of dealing with specific difficulties. In both instances (in the minis-

[7] From *Leaves of Grass*.

ter's knowledge of the private secrets of his people, and in his knowledge of how to deal with them) the pastor confronts the practical application of the principle of the love of Christ.

In the first place, people will not tell their pastor — or anyone else, for that matter — their inmost problems *for fear* they will be condemned. Also, they will not tell these noisome troubles *for fear* they will be exposed to others and confidences betrayed. These are the two great hindrances to the establishment of a relationship of a trusted motive. The process of reconciliation goes on between pastor and people as he gradually impresses them that Christian love lies in knowing each other even as they are known of God, and yet accepting each other as they are because God has so accepted them. Such love casts out fear. Therefore, love has no meaning apart from their personal knowledge of each other and from an ethically severe kind of forgiveness of each other's frailties. Jesus set the Christian fellowship in this framework when he said, " I am in the Father, the Father in me, and I in you." Paul aligns perfect love and perfect knowledge in the thirteenth chapter of I Corinthians, and in Phil. 1:9 he prays that " love may abound more and more, with knowledge and all discernment." Karl Menninger lays his finger on the same understanding when he says that

" Love is impaired by dread, more or less dimly felt by everyone, lest others see through our masks, the masks of repression that have been forced upon us by convention and culture. It is this that leads us to shun intimacy, to maintain friendships on a superficial level, to underestimate and to fail to appreciate others lest they come to appreciate us only too well. Love is experienced as pleasure in proximity, a desire for a fuller knowledge of one another, a yearning for mutual identification and personality fusion." [8]

Furthermore, the pastor's relationship may be impaired also if his parishioners suspect that he is using them as psychological cadavers on which to demonstrate his counseling techniques, rather than caring for them as a good shepherd does his sheep — with love and simplicity of motive. His very knowledge of human nature, if used

[8] *Love Against Hate,* p. 272. Harcourt, Brace and Company, 1942.

as an end in itself, may become an impediment to his usefulness. *Every knowledge of the human heart, every skill in dealing with human problems, is equally dangerous as it is useful, and ordinarily it is the presence or absence of the love of Christ that makes the difference.*

Therefore, the knowledge and the affections of a Christian pastor must be in harmony with each other. He can never hope to separate the principle of truth from the principle of love and still remind men and women of Jesus.

III. The Pastor as an Instrument of the Holy Spirit

" *While they were talking and discussing together, Jesus himself drew near and went with them.*" — *Luke 24:15.*

Jesus as the living Christ manifests himself vitally in the presence of the Holy Spirit. The Christian pastor does well to think of his face-to-face ministry to people as a form of prayer. As he and his people talk and discuss together, or for that matter simply sit in silence together, Jesus himself in the presence of the Holy Spirit according to his promise draws near and goes with them. This is a more adequate understanding of the place of prayer in pastoral work than to think of it as being limited to those formal occasions when he reads a part of the Scripture and bows or kneels in prayer with a person or a group of persons.

Such a feeling of being a continual instrument of the Spirit of God lends reverence to the pastor's interpersonal relationships, and naturalness and spontaneity to those special occasions when formal expressions of prayer are appropriate. Ministers who are allowed access to the secrets of human hearts are not immune to developing a raw sense of familiarity with the crudity and frailty of their fellow human beings. Likewise, ministers who are continually called upon for formal prayers are often led to the edge of profaning this holy experience by entering into it lightly, inappropriately, mechanically, and by carrying through with it without depth, sensitivity, or dignity. Furthermore, the seething mass of detail that calls for the concern of a busy pastor often disperses his attention in such a way that his pastoral work becomes corroded with a creeping sense of fatigue that brings inattention and boredom.

The only effective way a pastor can offset this raw sense of familiarity, this bordering upon the profaning of prayer, and this creeping sense of fatigue, inattention, and boredom is to consider each one of his personal interviews with people as an experience of prayer. A few ministers practice this, and one of them was described by one of his friends in this way: "When you are talking with him you have the feeling that for those few minutes or for that hour *you* are the *only* earthly concern that he has." This is filling one's ministry "with all the fullness of God."

The promises of Jesus concerning the Holy Spirit dispel all doubt concerning the intention of the Master as to the dependence of his disciples upon the Holy Spirit's use of them as instruments of his redemptive work. Pastors often long for a never-failing technique which they can use in any situation with success. Likewise they want to know *one* procedure to follow in dealing with all people who have a similar grouping of difficulties — such as divorcees or alcoholics. But each testing situation calls for different measures, indicated only by the pastor's sensitivity to and grasp of the need of the moment. The appropriateness of the moment determines what needs to be said and how it should be said. But it takes a restful relaxation given only by the Holy Spirit to lay aside all preconceived attacks. This may be a glimmer of the brilliant light Jesus gave his disciples in his assignment of pastoral duties: "Take no thought how or what ye shall speak: for it shall be given you in that same hour what ye shall speak. For it is not ye that speak, but the Spirit of your Father which speaketh in you" (Matt. 10:19, 20).

Furthermore, the Holy Spirit functions as Creator of community, as Luke puts it: "All who believed were together," as a result of the action of the Holy Spirit bringing about a sense of belonging and shared meaning between a pastor and his people. The Holy Spirit is the comforter who strengthens, given that he might "be with us." The Holy Spirit is the instructor, given that he might "teach . . . all things." The Holy Spirit is the convicter, who convicts of "sin and of righteousness and of judgment." The Holy Spirit is the healer who makes men whole by bringing to remembrance those spiritual reserves for combating psychological diseases. And finally, the Holy Spirit is the co-worker, who is with us always in the commissioned tasks of Christ.

These functions of the Holy Spirit become the tasks of the minister under the guidance of the Holy Spirit in his interpersonal relationships. At one time he is the *understanding friend* who works in the processes of fellowship, creating a sense of community, breaking down the middle walls of partition and developing a sense of togetherness with otherwise isolated, withdrawn persons who have been cut off from the land of the living. At another time, he is the *comforting strength* of a person in the midst of a bereavement, a frustrated or broken love affair, an unbearable pain because of the sins of parents, or the heavy demands of war. The isolating power of suffering is met by the knowledge of the Holy Spirit that gives the sufferer access to " the whole creation [that] has been groaning in travail together until now," and it is the same Spirit that gives expression to "those groanings which cannot be uttered." The pastor's knowledge of the wisdom and feelings of the ages stored in the Bible will make it possible for him to express his people's inmost feelings *for* them.

Again the pastor functions as a *teacher* who informs an ignorant mind, or who supplies the missing piece in an otherwise confused perspective. Here he accepts as a fact the religious illiteracy of the average person and draws upon his total store of knowledge: the rudiments of his own experience, the patience and comfort of the Scriptures, the example of great personalities, and his systematic knowledge of literature and human nature. At another time he is the *spiritual confidant,* and parent confessor, to whom the fearful and guilt-laden person confesses his intimate sin, thinking all the time that it is unbelievable that another human being can look with compassion upon him, to say nothing of receiving God's forgiveness.

Or, to those individuals who are enthralled in the worship of themselves, the pastor becomes the one who unshackles their experience of God from their concepts of themselves and sets them on the path of progressive spiritual growth. At even another time, the pastor functions as the *healer* who helps uncover and "bring to . . . re-membrance" those buried memories of the past that nevertheless create blind spots in the person's present view of life and cause him to stumble in his way. Here he functions as a reconciler of paradoxical and conflicting desires, and helps his people to assimilate undigested and unacceptable past experiences in such a way as to profit by them rather than become enslaved to them. Finally, the pastor functions alongside his people as a *co-worker* in the great enterprise of the Kingdom of God. He is a " comrade in a radiant pilgrimage " in which the special relationship between "those . . . of the household of faith " sustains him. Thus, all his planning, meeting, experimentation, and ways of doing things become the in-struments of "insightful" relationships to people. As Paul put it, " What you have learned and received and heard and seen in me, do; and the God of peace will be with you " (Phil. 4:9).

These functions of the pastor serve to alternate with each other from time to time. The spiritual appropriateness of this or that function is largely a matter of timing the needs of each psychological moment. Ecclesiastes has a remark about this time (Eccl. 3:1-11):

"For everything there is a season, and a time for every purpose under heaven: a time to be born, and a time to die; a time to plant, and a time to pluck up . . . ; a time to kill, and a time to heal; a time to break down, and a time to build up; a time to weep, and a time to laugh; . . . a time to rend, and a time to sew; a time to keep silence, and a time to speak; a time to love, and a time to hate. . . . God . . . hath made everything beautiful in its time: also he hath set eternity in their heart."

And the capacity to fit eternity to time depends upon the total store of accrued knowledge and experience of the minister, his intuitive insight into the basic difficulties the individual is up against, and the degree to which he has yielded himself to the Holy Spirit for spiritual sensitivity and understanding.

Thus the interpersonal relationships of a pastor with his people in the times of their suffering become a continuous experience of prayer in the Spirit of God. In this experience the inner life of those to whom he ministers is continually being opened to the healing love of God as the personality of the minister is continually being yielded to the outworking purposes of God. Thus even as Fra Angelico painted Madonnas and angels while upon his knees, so also the minister of the healing redemption of the gospel goes about the task of bringing its marvelous light to darkened consciences, its fortifying strength to those who are weak and have no might, and its releasing freedom to those who are clutched by fear, consumed in wrath, and enslaved by inordinate affections.

IV. The Pastor as a Representative of a Specific Church

" Then after fasting and praying they laid their hands on them and sent them off." — Acts 13:3.

A mixed emotion of uneasy satisfaction comes over most ministers when they realize that they symbolize and represent a *specific congregation of people.* The definite form of a pastor's ministry is affected greatly by the history, the traditions, the personal opinions, and even the passing whims of this group of people. The Christian pastor is called, not only to speak *to* this congregation in his preaching ministry, but also to speak *for* them in his individual and group counseling. He cannot go " off duty " from this responsibility; it is a twenty-four-hours-a-day, seven-days-a-week ministry. He finds also that he must represent his congregation to the rest of the community, and occasionally to protect his members from the rest of the community. He uses his staff of guidance on his flock, and quite often must use his rod of protection upon attacks from without. His problem is to know *when* to use *which* upon *whom!* No veteran minister will call this an easy problem.

Therefore, a Christian pastor, being invested with such a responsibility, must have confidence in his congregation; he must believe in their essential integrity. He must be committed with a clear conscience to the major objectives, principal teachings, and operational strategy of the church to which he accepts a call. The time to clarify this loyalty is *before* he agrees to become their leader. The wise pastor, upon having received overtures from a new congregation, seeking that he become their pastor, will take pains to acquaint himself with the history, traditions, and practices of the church. He will decide in advance whether or not he can be the community advocate for such a congregation. More care and concern at these formative stages of a pastoral relationship between a pastor and a church will lead to more wholeheartedness of service in the days to come. Such precautions will serve to prevent disillusionment among ministers and confusion in congregations.

This does not mean that a pastor should assume that he will not relate himself to a church that does not sign a " dotted-line " agreement to all his expectations. Rather, it means that he is willing to cast his lot with them as he finds them and to give himself to them in a loyalty that makes room for the progressive development of their corporate life together. This implies that the pastor needs a working concept of what a church actually *is* as well as an ideal concept of what a church as the Body of Christ *can* be.

The Christian pastor not only represents the welfare of the Christian community; he also is a sponsor of the individual rights and needs of the persons within the community. One of the unique distinctives of the work of a minister is that he represents *both* the individual *and* the social good of his people at the same time. Individual interests often threaten the safety of the group, and the corporate selfishness of the group often oppresses the welfare of the individual. The sensitive pastor is conscious of the power of the church to isolate an individual, and also of the intentness with which some individuals dominate the church until they must be isolated in order that the community may survive. Therefore, the good minister repeatedly evaluates afresh the resources and liabilities of his congregation. He understands the dynamics of group behavior as well as the motives of individual conduct. The opportunities for personal counseling that come to him will arise most often in connection with groups with which he has met. And, too, the structure of his relationship to an individual is greatly determined by the kind of affiliation that person has with the church which the pastor represents.[9]

---

[9] See Rudolph Wittenberg, *So You Want to Help People,* pp. 61–121, Association Press, and J. W. Klapman, *Group Psychotherapy. Theory and Practice,* pp. 8–11, Grune & Stratton, Inc., 1946.

A pastor, by virtue of his personal as well as economic dependence upon his congregation, ordinarily gives preference to persons and groups within his church as over against those who do not belong to that fellowship. The next group in order are the close relatives and friends of members of his congregation, regardless of their connection with his church. The pastor is most often criticized in this connection for being absent from his pulpit and community in order to do this or that service for some other church or organization. He may also be attacked for spending so much time in individual counseling with a few persons who may or may not be concerned with the life of the church that he neglects the needs of the large number of people who are members of his church. The ethical decisions that a pastor must make as to the use of time and energy along these lines are legion in number. But the way he makes these decisions is the stream bed along which his usefulness to his people either flows or evaporates.

CHAPTER III

THE PERSONAL QUALIFICATIONS OF THE PASTOR

The representative of God, the ambassador of Christ, the instrument of the Holy Spirit, and the emissary of a church, must be a qualified person. This requires unusual spiritual equipment and emotional stability.

The writers of the New Testament were zealous and enthusiastic when they spoke of the necessity of a man's being called to the ministry, but they were equally exacting in their requirements of those who were chosen for the task. It could be fitly spoken of the early churches that *many* were called to the task of an overseer of souls but few were chosen.

Early Christians were not vague in their statement of the personal qualifications of those into whose hands was committed the care of the flock of God. They did not leave this important decision entirely to the sentimental whims of men who aspired to the office. The responsibility was laid upon and taken seriously by the churches themselves. The writers of the Pastoral Epistles felt it necessary to describe in minute detail the qualifications that they themselves sought to incorporate into their own way of life and the high standards that they held for those who became their fellow workers. They were convinced of the nobility of their task.

Consequently, churches today have at hand in the New Testament (I Tim. 3:1-7; Titus 1:5-9; I Peter 5:1-4) the standards whereby they may judge a man's fitness as their pastor, and aspiring candidates for the ministry may judge themselves.

I. Above Reproach

A pastor should be a person who has earned the respect of his community; that is, he is above reproach, not having been laid hold of for disorderliness, indecency, and immodesty. This is not merely a matter of having kept up appearances before one's neighbors, but rather that a person has proved his own work before his community and actually merits the approval and acceptance of those about him.

Especially important is it that a man have the respect of non-Christians. I Timothy states it: " He must be well thought of by outsiders " (I Tim. 3:7). The purpose of this requirement is made plain: " In order that he may not be publicly exposed to abuse and affliction and fall into the snare of the slanderer." The man who is to bear witness to those who are outside must have lived convincingly before them, be above their reproach, and have their respect if he is to have any influence over them. This requirement points not only to the positive witness of the church to those outside, but also to the need for protecting the flock of God from those on the outside.

Of course, it is a common saying that unless a minister is maligned by sinners, and persecuted by the unrighteous, he does not truly have the first fruits of being called to the ministry. The " persecutory passages " of the Scripture and the fact that the Chief Shepherd was criticized for eating with publicans and sinners are cited as supporting evidence. Nevertheless, the fact remains that it was the religious people of Jesus' day who criticized his behavior, and neither those who believed on him nor those who were publicans and sinners. Those who were on the outside, the lost sheep of the house of Israel, never accused him of being one of them. Among these groups he was " above reproach."

The ever-present fact of gossip and slander in a community hovers like the humidity over the face-to-face ministry of a pastor to his people; he may become unaware of it, but he is never free from its influence. It necessitates his being above reproach himself; he must have brought his whole life under a finely balanced discipline lest he himself become a castaway.

II. Not a New Convert

The New Testament says plainly that a pastor should not be a new convert, a novice, a neophyte. Rather, he should be a seasoned veteran of the Christian way of life. No specific length of service as an active Christian is stated, but experience taught these early churches that a " newly planted " Christian had to be put to the test of time before being given the responsibility of the care of others.

One clear reason for this requirement was stated: " In order that he may not become puffed up with conceit and fall into the condemnation of the false accuser." The literal phrase for " puffed up with conceit " is " to be wrapped up in a cloud," or " beclouded with conceit." This word is used again in I Tim. 6:4, 5: " He is puffed up with conceit, he knows nothing; he has a morbid craving for controversy and for disputes about words, which produce envy, dissension, slander, base suspicions, and wrangling among men who are depraved in mind and bereft of the truth, imagining that godliness is a means of gain."

Accordingly, then, the course of experience through which a novice goes when he attempts the work of a pastor is after this order: He first is overwhelmed by the new sense of importance of the role into which he has been cast. He gets the same sense of competitive victory that made Paul feel that he had advanced beyond many of his own age, and caused him to become " extremely zealous." Then the new convert begins to realize his inadequacy and becomes very insecure in trying to discharge the new responsibilities that bear so heavily upon him. This prompts him " to put up a front," and to try to cover his ignorance with high-sounding words and obscure intellectualisms that confuse his listeners and hide the simplicity of the gospel. This cloud of confusion brings on divisions and wranglings among people who are also babes in the way of Christ. Party cries begin to be heard, and the more emotionally unstable people of the community begin to use the situation of godliness to see who can gain his own personal ends.

Such a course of development in the pre-Christian experience of Paul is possibly one of the reasons why, when he became a Christian, he " did not confer with flesh and blood, nor . . . go up to Jerusalem to those who were apostles before " him. Rather, he went to Damascus and Arabia, and it was three years before he even conferred with the leaders of the Christian way. Then again it was fourteen more years before he sought their approval (Gal. 1:14 to 2:1).

Such Biblical understanding merits the conclusion that one of the explanations of " split churches " and a multiplying number of rival sects in Christendom today is the spiritual immaturity of carelessly chosen pastors and leaders. They are cakes not turned, burned on one side and raw on the other. Attempts therefore to unite Christendom without getting back to this source of its divisions are futile indeed. These groups are set into motion by spiritually adolescent leaders with a thirst for power, and they can do more to shatter the unity of churches in a short while than mature leaders can undo in a long time.

This does not mean that a person's age should be the sole determinant of his selection as a pastor, for the Scriptures do not refer merely to chronological age but to spiritual maturity. It does mean, however, that a man should have achieved a sufficient degree of full-grownness as a Christian not to get lost in the cloud of his own conceits.

III. The Husband of One Wife

Two of the Pastoral Epistles (I Timothy and Titus) require that the pastor be the husband of one wife. This may be interpreted several ways. First, polygamy and concubinage were prevalent practices in the communities of which the early churches were a part, and the writers evidently were insisting that their leaders be an example of the Christian principles of monogamic marriage. They looked upon singleness of devotion to one marital partner as essential to the integration of personality alongside the necessity of singleness of devotion to one God. These two distinctives set the Christians apart, in glaring contrast, from their neighbors who practiced both polygamy and polytheism.

Secondly, this passage may be interpreted less directly to mean that the early Christians preferred a *married* minister to a single one. This was evidently prior to the ascetic development of a celibate ideal for pastors, and one wonders what a Catholic priest thinks when he comes to this text. Social pressures among Protestant churches

today almost demand of a minister that he be married. So universal
is this demand that occasionally theological students depend upon
this external motivation for the selection of a mate rather than upon
inner devotion to the woman they marry. Likewise, the pressure for
a *certain kind* of woman, with ability to be a sort of " assistant to the
pastor," occasionally dominates the marital choice of ministers to
such an extent that affection becomes a secondary consideration. But,
nevertheless, the main intention of the Scriptural requirement seems
to be that a minister *needs* a wife as his companion in the work of
the gospel, as his partner in the enjoyment of their mutually expressed sexual powers, and as his comrade in the adventure of
parenthood.

Thirdly, this passage may be interpreted in the light of another
prevalent social problem at the time of the writing: *divorce.* At this
point the application becomes most pertinent to present-day practice.
Divorced men are, in increasing numbers, applying to theological
seminaries for admission to prepare for the active pastorate. This
poses a thorny ethical problem for the individual men involved, for
theological faculties, for ordination councils, and for churches in
need of pastors.

The statements of Paul in I Cor., ch. 7, reflect that the early
churches were very tender and sensitive to the plight of people who
became involved in pagan marriages prior to having become Christians. They most certainly did not consider divorce or even remarriage as an unpardonable sin for which they would break fellowship
with an individual Christian.

However, the early Christians had a higher standard, and a seemingly legalistic attitude about divorced persons, especially those
who had remarried, becoming the shepherds of the rest of the
" flock of God." *By their word, no divorced man who had remarried
could hold such a place of responsibility.* This seems to be a harsh
measure, but the study of the present-day experience of divorced
men in the ministry vindicates it as the kindest measure in the long
run. The divorcee (whether he is remarried or not does not seem
to matter) is so consumed in his inner fears that he cannot do the
work of pastor. First, he wonders whether he should tell the church

about his divorce or withhold the information from them. If he tells them, he is always fearful of what his people think of him for being divorced. If he is not remarried, he also has an exceptional psychological struggle in controlling his sexual impulses, and becomes socially handicapped in his relationship to the women of his age to whom he ministers. Added to this are the wounded memories of his former wife that plague him. With all this he may have very little energy left for his work as a pastor.

From the point of view of the ordination councils and of the churches that need a pastor, experience has taught that only occasionally will a council ordain a divorced man. Furthermore, it is next to impossible for a divorcee to be called by a congregation, especially when there are so many happily married pastors available. All these psychosocial pressures under which divorced candidates for the ministry labor can add crippling psychosomatic illnesses and mental disorders to any instabilities that may already have been operative in causing the divorce in the first place. This is not to say that a divorced person cannot find a vocation of Christian helpfulness to people and serve as a faithful witness for Christ. Nor is this to say that anything other than a spirit of gentle restoration should be used in counseling such a man. It is to say, however, that Christian compassion for the man himself as well as reverent concern for the New Testament standards of the ministry call for a man who has made a success of his first marriage.

Finally, clinical experience in marriage and family counseling teaches one more thing about *how a pastor shall be related* to the woman to whom he is married. He is to be her *husband* in the fullest sense of the word, and to set an example before the men of his community in the way he loves and cares for his wife. He is to be related to his wife as a husband, and not as a little child is to his mother. He is to be related to her as a husband, and not as a father is to a little daughter. They should be related to each other as man and wife, and not as pastor and parishioner who are continually reminding each other of their rank. They should be related to each other as man and wife, and not as separate members of the staff of a church. These other functions certainly condition the life of a minister and his wife together, but in no instance should any one of them become the determinative pattern of their relationship.

IV. He Must Manage His Own Household Well

The New Testament writers seem to assume that if a pastor is the "husband of one wife," he will also be the parent of children. One of their criteria of judging the fitness of a man for the ministry was his success as a parent. They required of him, therefore, that he should have a finely balanced control of his own home, because "if a man does not know how to manage his own household, how can he care for God's church?" (I Tim. 3:5).

Many pastors have interpreted this to mean that they are to rule over their children with an iron hand, the clutching authority of which is never to be relaxed. Such men are often embarrassed to find late in life that their children rise up in rebellion at the tyranny of their father and reject not only him but his religion. Certainly the writers of this passage of the New Testament meant something more than and different from this interpretation. The larger Biblical context reveals a more adequate understanding.

In the first place, the patriarchal type of family organization in which these early Christians participated had its beginnings in the early Hebrew period when the father of the family was the only priest of the family. He was the representative of God to the family, and all that has been said concerning the pastor as a representative of God applies also to his relationship to his family. Accordingly, the exhortation found in I Peter 5:2, 3, may be paraphrased and applied to the pastor's relationship to his children without doing violence to the total Biblical context: "Act as a shepherd to your children, not as lording it over them, but as an example before them." In other words, the power whereby a minister maintains control over his children is the strength of the child's natural need to become like his father. He depends more on the persuasive pull of this need than he does on the coercive demand of an infallible parental authority.

Again, the Greek word for "manage" is derived from a word

which means literally "to stand over." It is followed in the text by a term that is translated "with all gravity." This word is derived from another word which means "to worship." The interpretation of the law of identification set forth earlier is applicable here. On the human level, the character of the child is shaped by the tie of identification between him and his parents. If this goes either to the extreme of stark fear of the parent or abject servility to the parent, the father, for all practical purposes, becomes the god, the object of the infantile worship of the child. Therefore, the child is instructed by Paul, "Obey your parents *in the Lord,* for this is right" (Eph. 6:1). The pastor rules over his children as a representative of God and "in the Lord," not capriciously and by virtue of his own infallibility. In so doing, he serves as a "molding influence" upon the life of his family. He depends more upon the affectionate management of his own relationship to his children than he does upon "pulling his rank" as a preacher on them.

Not only does the pastor exert a molding influence over his family by maintaining a loving tie of identification between himself and them, but he also serves as a "sieve" to protect his family from destructive outside influences. The children of a pastor can very easily become confused by the many voices of the congregation who seek to direct their path. The possibility of their own choices may be purloined away by the social pressure of the group which the pastor represents. The protective function, therefore, of the pastor as a parent often has to be applied to the congregation as well as to people who are not Christians. The pastor should always stand *between* his family and his church as a protector from many well-meaning "authorities" on child guidance, as well as a mediator of the more desirable graces of the Christian fellowship.

A third meaning of the requirement of effective parenthood that is laid upon a candidate for the ministry is embodied in the instruction to Timothy: "If a man does not know how to manage his own household, how can he care for God's church?" (I Tim. 3:5). The word translated "care for" is used only one other time in the New Testament. In Luke 10:34, 35, the word describes the way the good Samaritan treated the wounded man whom he found. Actually, then, it means in this context that the pastor cares for the church with a *healing carefulness*. The minister cares in the same manner for his children, supplying their economic and bodily needs as well as their spiritual ones. In another place, Timothy is instructed: " If any one does not provide for his relatives, and especially for his own family, he has disowned the faith and is worse than an unbeliever " (I Tim. 5:8).

This is not to say that a pastor is to let luxury and extravagance determine his ministry. It is to say, however, that real question may be raised as to the sincerity of a candidate for the ministry who uses his Christian calling as an excuse to neglect the basic physical and emotional needs of his children. If a man neglects his own children's needs for affectionate tenderness, spiritual instruction, and economic security, he will have no basis for a genuinely pastoral care of the flock of God.

An acid test of the fitness of a minister for his work is to be such a parent that his children can look up to him and want to be like him and his Lord. It reveals the connection between family maladjustment and the use of religion as an escapism from what would otherwise be an impossible home situation. The face-to-face ministry of a pastor to his people calls for the skills and patience of a successful parent. By and large, people react in most subsequent groups in much the same way they learned to react to their mothers and fathers, brothers and sisters.[10] They carry these established patterns with them into the rest of life. In the church, more often than not, the other members of the family are present also. This requirement of successful parenthood, then, is as old as the New Testament and as contemporary as some of the most recent research in psychology.

V. SANE, SENSIBLE, OF A SOUND MIND

The mental health of a man who aspired to the office of an overseer of souls was of concern to the early churches. Jesus himself was vitally concerned with people being " clothed and in . . . [their]

[10] S. R. Slavson, *The Practice of Group Therapy,* pp. 219 ff. International Universities Press, 1948.

right mind." He gave himself to the healing of those who were de-
mented and stimulated the compassion of his disciples then and now
to bring the therapeutic power of the Christian gospel to bear upon
life situations. But when he had healed such persons, though they
" begged that . . . [they] might be with him . . . he sent . . .
[them] away, saying, ' Return to your home, and declare how much
God has done for you ' " (Luke 8:38 f.). He did not choose them for
the places of heaviest responsibility. Their best witness was as well
persons in their home community, now that they were healed.

The Epistles of Timothy and Titus both use the same term which
may be translated variously as " sane," " sensible," or " of a sound
mind," " self-controlled," " sober-minded." Those words from which
it is derived, and those words to which it is related, refer unmistak-
ably to the emotional stability of the candidate for the ministry. The
writers specify the several different ways they judged the mental
health of a candidate:

First, he must be a person whose moral sensitivity has not been
dulled and gapped by the use of alcohol. He cannot be a person
who " spends his time sitting by a bottle." The lowered threshold of
moral sensitivity, the shaken loss of physical precision, and the
aching emptiness of unrequited anxieties so characteristic of the
person who solves his problems with alcohol are all counterindica-
tions as to his fitness for the ministry to other people. He stands in
need of a physician himself, and will most certainly pass his neurotic
way of life on to someone else.

Secondly, he must also have control of his desire for money. He
cannot be a person who is avaricious for gain, and whose simplicity
of devotion to the care of the flock is adulterated by the worship of
accumulated money. He cannot serve two masters, God and mam-
mon. He cannot bypass as of secondary importance the primary con-
cerns of human need and the edification of the mental and spiritual
lives of his people in order to achieve his own financial ends.

Thirdly, the pastor must have control of his desire for power. His
prestige-seeking impulse must not be so out of proportion to his
other spiritual hungers that he feels that he must " lord it over " his
flock and squelch anyone who dares compete with him or oppose

him. He cannot push his own needs for independence of his people so far that he does not recognize his independence upon them for that reasonable degree of approval that makes for mental health and social usefulness. He cannot succeed in such a manner that he causes one of his " little ones " to fail.

Fourthly, most emphasis, however, is placed upon the degree of mastery a man has over his temper. Titus says that he should be a " master of himself." This implies that he has great strength and power of spirit, but he knows how to express his aggressions in a positive and healthy manner. He is not " arrogant " and self-pleasing, inclined to orgies of bad temper in which he delivers himself over to his own meanness of spirit. He is not " violent but gentle," not " quarrelsome," and continually searching out something over which to start a fight. He may be described also as a " noncombatant " in the fights which those around him choose to start. In a word, the pastor does not label his own lack of self-control as his " prophetic ministry," and is keenly conscious of the fact that he " prophesies in part."

The absence of these negative factors does not attest to the mental health of a person unless certain positive values live in their place. Therefore, the writers specify that a pastor needs a well-balanced sense of moderation, rather than to be given to extremisms. His sense of fairness and appreciation of fitting behavior appropriate to each occasion reflect the precision of his self-control. Titus calls this " being just," or " rendering to every man his due because of his own uprightness." Matthew Arnold most aptly described this fine mental balance as " sweet reasonableness." The mentally healthy person is the one who has a reasonable degree of insight into his own weaknesses and has learned to turn them to the best advantage. He has the capacity for bearing a reasonable amount of frustration of his own desires, for sensing other people's privations before deploring his own, and for accepting responsibility for his own thoughts, decisions, and actions.

The New Testament writers tend to interpret mental stability in terms of self-control. This is something very different from repression as described by the psychologists, which, as Sigmund Freud has said, lies "simply in the function of rejecting or keeping something out of consciousness." Repression consists of an unawareness that one even has inordinate aggressions, in which case the person may feign humility in such a way that it angers all those around him. But self-control consists of the frank recognition of one's hungers and impulses and the acceptance of the personal responsibility for their management.[11]

Mission boards have realized the importance of the requirement of a high degree of emotional stability for appointees to foreign service, and have enlisted the aid of personality tests and psychiatric examinations of the candidates. More recently, some denominations, especially the Episcopalians and Presbyterians, have begun specific programs for the strengthening of the mental health of candidates for their parish ministry. Much effort is being made to guide those persons who have "severe personality disturbances which may cause difficulty to themselves and embarrassment to the Church" into other vocations than the ministry.[12] Admissions committees in theological seminaries are gradually becoming aware of the necessity for psychological screening of applicants. Professors Guiles and Billinsky at Andover Newton Theological School have devised a special test which is given to all applicants for admission to that school. Although these beginning steps toward promoting a high standard of mental health for candidates for the ministry are heartening, there is a real need for younger ministers to conduct a voluntary search for guidance. A young minister preparing for this noble task should systematically set about the business of removing emotional weights that so easily beset him and render him ineffective or positively harmful in his personal ministry to people. The most natural way of accomplishing this is to turn to older ministers and theological professors who have devoted their lives, not only to their own active ministry, but also to the careful training of other ministers. Another way is to serve "apprenticeship" pastoral functions alongside spirit-

---

[11] Sigmund Freud, "Repression" (1915), *Collected Papers,* Vol. IV, p. 86. Hogarth Press, Ltd., 1948.

[12] Clifford E. Davis, *Counseling the Candidate, Psychological Techniques in Recruiting Church Leadership,* p. 4. Board of Christian Education of the Presbyterian Church in the U. S. A., 1949.

ually healthy ministers from whom one can learn. Then too the growing facilities for the clinical training of theological students provide controlled conditions whereby a prospective minister can face the hidden anxieties in his own personality as he ministers to large numbers of institutionalized people.

If a prospective minister discovers that he is using more energy fighting his inner conflicts than he is in doing the work of the Lord, if he senses that his personal relationships to his family and his associates are such that they prevent him from being an " able minister of the new testament," he should feel no embarrassment about searching out a qualified Christian physician who can render him whatever therapy is needed. A good majority of personality handicaps *can be overcome,* given a spirit of teachableness on the part of the afflicted person. The minister-to-be should not expect to solve *all* his personal problems *before* he attempts to deal with those of others. This is a fantasy in itself. He will do well to have dealt adequately with his major handicaps by the time he starts his active and full-time ministry.

Churches seeking pastors are most in need of education along the line of choosing men who are spiritually healthy. The size of a man and the sound of his voice are not adequate standards for judging this. The New Testament, as has been seen in this context, speaks with definiteness and accuracy on the things to look for in a minister's personal stability. The churches are under obligation to " try every spirit " to see whether it is of God, because there are many false prophets gone out into the world. The true prophet needs all the fiber of personality he can muster to stand the test of the pastoral relationship. False prophets often find their ways most easily into the affections of their people by reason of their " standing head and shoulders above the rest," their speaking " in the tongues of men and of angels," or their compulsive zeal which " scours land and sea." Only when the churches demand something better will ministers be chosen who are capable of bringing health as well as goodness, soundness of mind as well as strength of zeal, and wholesomeness of direction as well as intentness of purpose to the life of the Body of Christ.

VI. He Must Have a Firm Hold on the Sure Word

The emotional stability of a minister has a great deal to do with the quality of his beliefs and largely determines the manner in which he seeks to impart these beliefs to others. Therefore, the New Testament writer insists that he have a firm hold on the sure word of the gospel. He must have a sense of certainty about the truths he teaches and the Person whom he represents. As Washington Gladden has so appropriately said:

"The existence of the spiritual realm and the main facts of that realm are the postulates of the pastor's problems. That love and not law is at the heart of the universe; that there is a conscious God, our Father, who loves men and seeks their welfare; that between the spirit of man and the Spirit of God there may be fellowship and communion, so that light and help and peace and power can flow from the grace that abounds to the need that implores; that man is a free spirit whose choice determines his destiny — all this is assumed. Any man who is in doubt on any of these propositions stultifies himself by accepting the office of a pastor. His problem is not to assure himself of these things, but to bring them home to the lives of men." [13]

The pastor must be competent to give his people a sense of certainty about their life in relationship to God, because, as Paul has said: "If the trumpet give an uncertain sound, who shall prepare himself to the battle?" (I Cor. 14:8). Two evident reasons support such a demand upon the pastor: first, people depend upon their pastor for confidence, security, and certainty amid suspicion, insecurity, and doubt. As Goethe appealed, so do they: "Give me your convictions; I need them. Keep your doubts; I have enough of my own." Secondly, every congregation has a legitimate need for authority in its minister. He must be able to speak as one having authority within his own personal experience with Christ, within the thoroughness of his knowledge of the record of revelation, within the firsthandness of his own understanding of human nature, and within the intimacy of his own acquaintance with grief and pain. Such an authority meets a group's needs, whereas the traditions of the scribes leave them thirsty.

[13] *Op. cit.,* p. 93.

VII. A Healthy Teacher

Again the minister is expected not only to have a firm hold on his beliefs as a Christian, but to have laid hold of a healthy quality of teaching. He needs to be a mature man in Christ who is no longer "tossed to and fro and carried about with every wind of doctrine, by the cunning of men, by their craftiness in deceitful wiles" (Eph. 4:14). He is to have a firm hold on the sure word that is taught in order that he may give instruction "in the health-giving doctrine." Paul especially was aware of the fact that many congregations of people do not want a man of stability; they prefer the unstable pastors. He said, "Having itching ears they will accumulate for themselves teachers to suit their own likings, and will turn away from listening to the truth and wander into myths" (II Tim. 4:3, 4).

Titus saw that teaching is the Church's most effective means of producing spiritually healthy people, and that it plays the same part in the life of those who are whole that healing takes in the life of those who have need of a physician. This gives a vital significance to the original meaning of "orthodoxy." From the point of view of Titus, orthodoxy is that kind of teaching which creates wholeness of life in an individual's relationships to himself and to his fellows by reason of his firmer hold upon the reality of God in Christ. From the point of view of the individual, the soundness of a teaching may be determined by its influence upon the forces of spiritual growth within the life. From the point of view of the group life of the church, the soundness of a teaching may be determined by whether or not it contributes to the "edification of the church." If a teaching confirms childish irresponsibility in an individual, and justifies that person in remaining just as he is with no need for teachableness and no confession of the need for growth, it can be justly called unsound. If a teaching or a practice divorces a group of people from a Christlike spirit and alienates them from one another and the larger community of Christians, genuine question may be raised as to its soundness.

VIII. An Apt Teacher

The New Testament writers expect of pastors, not only that they be sure of their teaching and that the quality of their teaching be sound, but that they be capable of making these teachings come alive to their people. The pastor must be an " apt teacher."

The aptitude of a minister for his task is one sure evidence of God's intention in his life, because God does not call a person to do something without reference to his own creative gifts to that person in the first place. Colloquially, the word " apt " has a curious double meaning. It is often used to mean " likely to come to pass." In this context, the question could be asked concerning a candidate for the ministry: " Is this person likely to function with success in the role to which we are setting him apart? " Then, again, the word " apt " is often used to mean " capable, or possessing the ability " to teach. Much research needs to be done and clear instruction given by already active pastors as to the specific skills necessary for competent action as a minister. The Spirit of God always takes the form of the vessel which it fills, and the specific form which the sense of mission takes in an individual's life is largely determined by his basic intelligence and his vocational aptitudes.

This matter has been left to chance and to the competitive struggle for existence among the churches and among ministers. A natural law of selection works in weeding out incompetent men, but it works apart from the loving intelligence of Christian people and is often a cruel thing in its operation. The end results of wasted human lives because of prayerless and careless vocational choices and irresponsible spiritual guidance on the part of pastors who counsel young people about entering the ministry have been bitter disappointments. The sight of a thirty-year-old man who has spent half of his life in school preparing for the ministry, and finally ekes out a living selling encyclopedias would frighten his earlier spiritual guides. Many are called into the ministry without a full knowledge of its demands. The blight of disappointment sets in when they, by their own word, conclude that they will never be capable of doing the work of a pastor.

Wise counsel suggests that spiritual appeals for life dedications to Christian work should be made in such a way as to allow room for the processes of time, growth, and spiritual instruction to fit the intentions of the consecrated person to the realistic objectives which he is actually capable of achieving. This would involve a deepened and broadened understanding of " the glory of God in the Christian calling." It would also involve a step-by-step path of preparation and decision rather than a one-leap approach. Some sensitive spirits find their place in the world in a moment, in a twinkling of an eye, but they are the rare ones rather than the customary ones. Therefore, to make a wholesale, detailed, specific dedication which one finds out later he has neither the ability nor opportunity to realize may actually do a person harm. Nevertheless, to move under the sealed orders of one's Lord may call for equally as much faith and reward one with equally as much adventure.

IX. WORKING NOT BY CONSTRAINT BUT WILLINGLY

The next standard that is set forth in I Peter for a minister is that he be spontaneously happy in his work. This is one sure test of the call of God to a work: the degree of peace and satisfaction one has in doing the work. The shepherd is enjoined in I Peter 5:2-4 to do his work not out of a dull sense of necessity and morbid compulsion but of his own free will and desire. This cuts across the grain of much conviction that men must have " fought the call " to be a minister, and that after having submitted they would be doing something else if they had their own choice in the matter.

Then, too, the shepherd is encouraged to maintain a sense of spiritual anticipation and eagerness in turning off his work, rather than to look upon his work as a " professional service rendered " for which the congregation " owes " him his pay. There is a vast difference between the shepherd and the hireling. The one enters into a creative fellowship with the Chief Shepherd, and the other is counting the hours until payday and wondering whether those who came in later than he did are getting as much pay as he is. The one has a sense of mission and the other has a job.

A servile attitude of a hireling is naturally followed by an increasing necessity to "lord it over" the flock. Then there is no spontaneous joy in a pastor's work and when there is a fleecing attitude on the pastor's part, the people soon begin to rebel against him. Then he becomes anxious, irritable, and unhappy, because no dictator can be otherwise. He is always afraid lest his authority be questioned, challenged, defied, or betrayed, and he has to depend upon a "gestapo" that he cannot trust to enforce his commands. A happy pastor, though, is the one who depends upon his affectionate ties with his people for the force of his leadership. He depends not upon the love of power, but the power of love for the achievement of results — not as "domineering over" those in his charge, but as an example to the flock.

The pastor's love, however, is not sufficient. That cannot be his crown of glory. Rather, the consummate requirement of him is that he depend devotedly upon the Chief Shepherd for his own spiritual sustenance and live in the buoyant expectation of his continual manifestation of himself. Titus calls this being "holy" and "a lover of goodness." These terms of endearment of the life of a pastor lay the emphasis upon his consecration and devotion, without which all other qualifications are in vain and usually are consumed in their own vanity. Sören Kierkegaard has called this "purity of heart," by which he means the power "to will one thing, and that is Christ."

The pastor cannot haggle with halfheartedness, partializing of desires, reservations of mind. Having brought all mixed emotions and ambivalent feelings to consciousness, he has dealt with them to a positive conclusion. The multiplicity of selves which cast a vote in the congress of this man's destiny must have cast their "Yes!" in favor of the noble task of the pastor. Then the man is ready for his work as a good minister of Jesus Christ, capable of standing and having stood all to stand. He can say with Walter Rauschenbusch: "I have found a task apart from which nothing I have ever learned or done is foreign."

CHAPTER IV

THE TOTAL TASK OF THE PASTOR

The Christian minister's task is a single labor, but it involves diverse responsibilities. A natural unity binds the pastoral task of a minister to his work as a religious educator, as a preacher, and as a leader of worship. These functions cannot be separated from each other. They are the separate facets of the same jewel, interrelated to each other and reflecting their beauty and light back and forth upon each other.

The pastor needs a unified, *total view* of his work as a whole. If he does his work well, he needs the refreshing strength that comes from seeing his task as an integrated and balanced whole, rather than as the divided camp of contradictory demands which it often appears to be. Such an expanded perspective must have been sustained by Jesus through the medium of his own worship life during those times when he would draw apart from even his own disciples for the renewing wholeness that comes from worship.

At the same time, however, the total task of the minister needs analysis, also, through which the face-to-face ministry to individuals may be seen as it is related to the pastor's function as a religious educator, as a preacher, and as a leader of public worship.

I. Religious Education and the Pastoral Task

The group life of the church as a teaching agency of the community is intimately related to the pastoral care and personal counseling which the pastor does. The pastor cannot relegate the educational life of the church to an assistant without doing violence to both his preaching and his pastoral relationship. The education that a congregation receives through the church school provides the background of understanding with which they hear a pastor preach. It serves as a front line of preventive defense against those conflicts which cause people to seek pastoral counseling. The reasons for this are not so evident and need clarification, however.

The pastor who takes his parishioners' personal problems seriously finds himself overwhelmed by the many individuals both within and without his congregation who seek help. He cannot possibly get to them all. He finds himself in need of getting persons with similar difficulties and needs together in groups in order that he may more adequately serve them in those needs which can be dealt with on a group level. For instance, many pastors have discovered that a wholesome group life cushions the shock to retirement for older people and keeps them from becoming ingrown in their later years. " Group work with, and pastoral care of, older people are complementary ways by which the church and pastor minister to those in later maturity. No pastor can make a choice between them. He must use both." [14] This could also be said of the other age groups and interest groups of the church.

Again, the educational life of the church gives the pastor access to the families of the individuals who seek his counsel. The taproot of the unhappiness of the individuals with whom a pastor counsels is in their family relationships. A pastor spends great parts of each week in marriage and family counseling. To conduct such a program of pastoral care and personal counseling without an adequate curriculum in family life education, with which to prevent such difficulties and to do away with the need for counseling, is gross pastoral nearsightedness. The training of young people, not only in the dramatic story and ethical imperatives of the Bible, but also in the preparation for and participation in Christian marriage, is an indispensable part of the pastoral care and personal counseling of a pastor.

Furthermore, an adequate educational program provides both an inlet and an outlet for pastoral care and personal counseling. For instance, from two contacts with a discussion group on the subject " Learning Spiritual Values in Family Living " a pastor received

[14] Paul B. Maves and J. Lennart Cedarleaf, *Older People and the Church,* p. 155. Abingdon-Cokesbury Press, 1949.

three requests from individuals attending the group for counsel concerning their family problems. One was an impending divorce situation, another a case in which a marriage had been consummated under false pretenses, and another a family in which the presence of the parents of both the man and the wife in their home was gradually stifling the growth of the children. Likewise, in this same group were several couples with whom the pastor had already counseled in premarital guidance, two of whom had invited the pastor to perform their wedding ceremony for them. The fact that educational groups serve as an inlet through which people may come to a pastor for individual help and an outlet with which he can conserve the results of his personal counseling makes his educational program of primary concern to him. To neglect the educational program of the church or to relegate it to others without concern is to lose touch with one of the main sources of counseling opportunities.

The pastor is largely responsible for the selection of lay leadership in the educational program of the church. At this point his counseling function and his work as a religious educator converge most meaningfully.

Whatever methods the churches of various denominations have of recruiting lay workers in the educational life of the church, one need remains constant: *These persons should be emotionally healthy in addition to being willing to serve.* Religious work meets many inner needs of persons: relief from guilt, escape from home tensions and conflicts, relief from boredom, and other security needs. These needs, however, should be secondary to the welfare of the persons whom a Sunday school teacher seeks to guide. Quite often the parishioner who is most eager to gain or to retain a church office is the least competent to do the work.

Therefore, leaders should be chosen carefully and close attention should be given to the personal adequacy and emotional stability of persons who volunteer for a given task. This can be done tactfully through home visitation and personal counseling. One church in the acquaintance of this author consistently follows this practice and the result has been a healthy church with a minimum of inner conflict and friction between its organizations.

Thirdly, the family life of parishioners and their group life in the church are psychologically and educationally separate facets of the same experience. The marital and parental happiness of the leaders of the church becomes a contagion for good or evil in the younger members who follow their patterns of living. Therefore, the pastor needs to work for the selecting of leaders who have adequately succeeded as parents and as participating members of families. Such leaders can sponsor a strong curriculum in family life education. Healthy leadership and an adequate church school curriculum become bonds that tie the pastoral task and the educational work of a minister together in an inseparable union.

II. Preaching and the Pastoral Task

Vital contrasts distinguish the preaching ministry from the pastoral task. Elaboration of each of these distinctives will add strength to this meaning.

The preaching ministry is a public one; the pastor's access to the crowd is emphasized. But the pastoral task is ordinarily a private and personal ministry, and the relative anonymity of the service is emphasized. This difference is accentuated when a parishioner fears that confidences given to a minister in private may become topics and illustrations for his preaching in public. The pastor often discovers as he counsels with a parishioner that the person feels as though he were being singled out in certain statements made in a sermon.

Furthermore, many people prefer to talk with a minister whom they do not see every Sunday and who does not know all their friends than to talk with their own pastor. This may be true even though these persons have no fear of or lack of confidence in their own pastor. The chaplain in the hospital observes this in remarks that patients make about their pastors. As one lady said: "I could never tell my pastor these things. He knows me too well. But I can tell them to a chaplain, because he is detached." The pastoral relationship, in its deeper reaches, requires a considerable degree of anonymity in order that the person may be aided in the difficulties that matter most to him.

This calls for extensive co-operation among ministers of the same community in referring persons who are too close to them to other pastors who can maintain a more detached and objective relationship. It also necessitates a close co-operation between the pastor and medical doctors who are skilled in counseling people. In larger communities, pastoral referral centers and pastoral counseling centers have been and will continue to be established. Specialized help of skilled psychologists of religion and pastoral counselors is slowly becoming a felt need in a few communities.

The second distinction between the pastoral and the preaching situations is the time element. Pastoral work is difficult to control in terms of the extent of time needed for individuals and of the number of persons who seek the pastor's help. The pastoral care and personal counseling ministry of a pastor can so encroach upon his time that he will have time for nothing else. This in turn becomes a barrier to effective pastoral counseling, because people will feel so guilty about taking the pastor's time that their qualms of conscience will prevent them from using wisely the time that he does give them. A vicious circle is set up that only a vacation will break! Conversely, the time element enters again when the pastor, pressed for the preparation of the sermon for Sunday, is interrupted by a person who needs immediate attention. The minister may have difficulty listening to the person's story, and may even be tempted to preach to the parishioner what little of the sermon he has prepared.

Again, the preaching-pastoral relationship proposes a paradox in the approach that a minister uses to the needs of the same people. As a preacher, he approaches their lives in terms of goals, ideals, objectives, and purposes for living in the Kingdom of God. But in pastoral care and personal counseling, the pastor approaches people, not merely as one who is unswervingly loyal to the absolute ideals of Jesus, but also as one who understands when people miss the mark of the ideals of Jesus. As a pastor, he has the wisdom of the serpents concerning the frailties of human nature and an affectionate tenderness that will " lift up the fallen." Pastoral leadership casts its light in the arc of these two poles of influence: the devotion of a pastor to the absolute ideals of Jesus and the patience of a pastor with human imperfection. The preaching task is primarily that of challenging men with the distant and flickering but unquenchable lights of the City of God; the pastoral task is primarily that of being able to identify with people just as they are, " to sit where they sit," even in their " haunts of wretchedness " in the cities of men " where cross the crowded ways of life." The two functions are coalesced in the worship of God as the minister learns himself to participate with his congregation in the processes of growth in the covenant of the loving ideals of Jesus.

Enough of the distinctions between a minister's preaching function and his pastoral task have been named to impress upon a minister the difficulty of his total work. However, some startling parallels between the two relationships ease the adjustment considerably. The similarities outweigh the difficulties.

The good preacher depends upon the same laws of personality as does the good pastor for the effectiveness of his work. The dynamics of preaching, teaching, and healing are much the same as far as the pastor's relationship is concerned. For instance, in pastoral care and personal counseling, the pastor must establish a " relationship of a trusted motive," before the person can be helped by him. He must be able to put himself in the place of the individual with whom he is counseling. In turn, that person must be able " to identify " with the pastor, i.e., to trust his motives, appreciate his way of life, and even desire to be like him. The establishment of this rapport takes time and patient relaxation of suspicions and defenses of all kinds.

This is equally true of the relationship of a preacher to a congregation. A bond of honor and shared feeling transmits the message of a preacher to a people. Some pastors can establish this more quickly than others, but the sense of togetherness must be there before the sermon becomes a reality to the hearers. The congregation tests the reality of a man's utterance without planning to do so, and the sermon becomes an " I-Thou " relationship, a personal encounter, as Farmer (following Martin Buber) has accurately said.[15]

[15] H. H. Farmer, *The Servant of the Word,* p. 56. Charles Scribner's Sons, 1942.

Preaching as a personal encounter becomes the careful and devoted management of a growing understanding between a pastor and his congregation rather than merely an oratorical demonstration. The theological professor who has been a pastor and blended his mind with that of a congregation finds occasional preaching in first one pulpit and then another to a group of total strangers to be a tasteless experience in comparison. Pastoral care and personal counseling lend feeling and meaning to preaching. Preaching becomes the preparation for counseling.

As such, the preaching of a sermon becomes an inlet into counseling with individuals, an important source of precounseling contacts. Also, the ministry of comfort and reassurance, instruction and interpretation, can often be done more powerfully through preaching than through individual counseling, because it is done in the presence of the larger community of worshipers. Having done this, a pastor in private conference with parishioners can spend his time in listening to their side of the story. Such a reciprocal relationship between pastoral care and preaching will go far in alleviating the feeling that many lay people express when they object to not being allowed to answer the preacher back or to ask him a question. A listening pastor makes an understanding preacher.

The pastor who maintains a consistent counseling ministry will move in the direction of a type of preaching that has been called "therapeutic preaching." The objective of such preaching is fourfold: (1) the *interpretation* of human experience in the light of Biblical truth rather than the exhortation of people to the observance of certain moral precepts, as such; (2) the development of personal *insight into the motives of personal and group action* rather than the condemnation of this or that kind of behavior; (3) the *encouragement* of the congregation toward faith in God, in one another, and in themselves as means of gaining control over behavior which they themselves discover to be alien to the mind of Christ; (4) the growth of *a sense of comradeship with God in Christ* and the changing of personality through this "transforming friendship."

Of course, this objective of therapeutic preaching is immediately identifiable as "the psychological approach" to homiletics. Such an objective implies a *conversational, eye-contact, extemporaneous delivery* rather than a more impersonal, formal, and oratorical delivery. It rules out histrionics and other appeals to the more superficial emotions that are united to the sense of touch, sound, and rhythm. It calls for a personal inventory, a confrontation of the self, and a reordering of the deep emotions of family love and hate, vocational intention, and the fundamental desires that drive human action.

Naturally, therapeutic preaching produces rest from tension through the resolution of conflict and the relief from a sense of guilt. It stands over against the type of preaching that creates unrest through the introduction of conflict into a complacent mind and the development of a sense of guilt in people who are " past feeling " a given moral or spiritual value. As such, a sermon based on the therapeutic objective qualifies as an act of worship in itself. The people of God are refreshed on their way.

Some have called this kind of preaching a type of pastoral care and personal counseling on a group level. A minister would make a mistake to give this ministry as a regular Sunday-after-Sunday diet for his congregation. Rather, he should incorporate it along with the other kinds of preaching and not become a slave to it or any other monotone in his preaching objectives.

III. Worship and the Pastoral Task

The relationship of a pastor to individuals, groups, and congregations undergoes a metamorphosis in the act of worship. Consciousness of his presence fades out and awareness of the real presence of God reaches its zenith. The quantitative differences of character between the pastor and those to whom he ministers become as nothing as the eternal qualitative difference between all men and God becomes more evident. The act of worship, therefore, has a wealth of connotations for the pastoral task of the minister.

Informal worship, where two or three are gathered together in the spontaneity of the shared knowledge of the presence of God, is the true atmosphere of the face-to-face relationship of a minister to an individual. The reverent care of living persons is a type of worship in its own right. This has been the primitive foundation of many religions, and, with all its limitations, is the extent of the worship of the vast majority of the people of the world. However, even in the Christian experience of worship, the reverence for God and the reverence for human personality are inseparable. The acute need of a suffering person is the medium of revelation most often promised by Jesus: "When did we see thee?" is the question of both true and insincere worshipers. "As you did it to one of the least of these my brethren, you did it to me." (Matt. 25:40.)

Although the face-to-face ministry of a pastor to individuals should be, and often is, an Emmaus road form of prayer, it does not become such without personal discipline on the part of the pastor. The question regularly comes to a pastor: "To whom do you go when the worries of other people become too heavy for you?" The answer to this question in a pastor's private worship life is the beginning of his own response to "a serious call to a devout and holy life." As Thomas a Kempis said: "No man doth safely speak, but he that is willing to hold his peace. No man doth safely appear abroad, but he who can gladly abide at home, out of sight. No man can safely command others but he that hath learned willingly to obey." The therapeutic power of Jesus came through prayer and self-discipline, and the modern pastor cannot expect it to be otherwise with himself.

The pastor who considers his interpersonal work of healing as a form of prayer in itself finds personal resources that keep his confidence in people strong, prevent him from losing patience with them, and undergird him with a steady calmness in the presence of acute pain and unhappiness. Without this sense of worship, the pastor becomes threadbare in the wear and tear of the emotional tension of his task. Fatigue sets in, irritability increases, aggressiveness and defensiveness are the next to follow. In order to allay his own sense of guilt, he then becomes overconcerned and overprotective toward those to whom he ministers. Consequently, he will spend more and more time with fewer and fewer people, and lose his perspective of even their needs.

Another connection between informal worship and pastoral work is apparent. The pastor's capacity to listen to people is dependent upon his own teachableness and his reverence for them. He cannot give such concern unless he has received it himself as an act of grace from God and those persons who nurtured him. The surplus of God's grace abounds to meet the needs of others. The Christian shepherd must necessarily be one whose "cup runneth over." Without this awesome sense of gratitude, without this sense of the abundance of the fullness of God in the satisfaction of his own needs, the pastor himself becomes demanding. He feels misunderstood and imposed upon. He feels like telling his own troubles to the person who is seeking his help. He becomes more talkative, and, with this, his capacity to listen has failed him. He becomes inattentive and insensitive to the subtle feelings of the person who seeks his help.

The third tie that binds worship to pastoral calling and counseling is the expectancy and need of people. The pastor who does not share in worship with those with whom he works soon begins to lose their respect. They begin to suspect his motives and to doubt his sincerity. A prayerless relationship between a pastor and his parishioners gradually relegates him either to the familiarity of all the rest of their social companions or to the chilly professionalism of an interviewer-client relationship. Both of these latter relationships have their intrinsic values, but they are peripheral to the central function of the minister as a representative of God.

Public worship, as indeed is true of private worship, likewise affords necessary resources for the conservation and multiplication of the pastoral effectiveness of a minister. One of the main distinctives of the role and function of the Christian pastor is that he is related to those whom he helps both individually and socially, both privately and publicly, both on horizontal planes of fellowship between man and man and on a vertical plane of communion between man and God. The place of public worship is where all these lines of influence and relationship meet.[16] Therefore, the minister has at his disposal the resources of the community of worship to meet the needs of the individual for worship and relief from isolation. The resources of the individual are at his disposal, also, to guide him toward the beautifica-

[16] O. J. Hodges, "The Distinctive Role of the Minister in Psychotherapy," unpublished thesis, Southern Baptist Theological Seminary, 1948.

tion of worship and the strengthening of the moral fiber of the community.

The objectives of public worship are almost synonymous with the objectives of good pastoral care and personal counseling. *Rest, the renewal of strength and energy through relaxation, is one of the shared objectives of both pastoral work and public worship.* The release from nervous tension and the discovery of new reserves of power for living through worship is a neglected emphasis in the activism of many Protestant churches. "Even the youths shall faint and be weary, and the young men shall utterly fall: but they that wait for the Lord shall renew their strength; they shall mount up with wings as eagles; they shall run, and not be weary; they shall walk, and not faint." (Isa. 40:30, 31.) This need prompted the institution of the Sabbath, sustains the continued practice of public worship, and vitally relates that practice to the healing ministry of the pastor.

The need for community in a sense of the shared meaning of life with others is also a common venture that prompts people both to participate in public worship and to seek the understanding counsel of their pastor. The pastor is the chosen representative of that specific community, and to converse with him personally is a private way of approaching that community. The relief from isolation through public worship with the people in Christ is the heart hunger of the worshiper's motive.

Sin and guilt isolate a person from those of his own community. They are accompanied by a longing for restoration "by those who are spiritual," for a sense of belonging again to the group whose approval is most important to the sinner, as well as restoration to God who insists upon clean hands and a pure heart in those who "worship him in spirit and in truth."

The private confession of sin has very little meaning apart from the corporate worship between imperfect people and the God and Father of the Lord Jesus Christ. These persons in turn are people of unclean lips also, and the individual lives in the midst of a people of unclean lips. All sin is a shared guilt as well as an individual responsibility before God. Corporate worship is God's remedy for cor-

porate sin. Here a person realizes that he is not alone in his sinful-
ness nor in his dependence upon the forgiveness of God. "All we
like sheep have gone astray; we have turned every one to his own
way" (Isa. 53:6) is an accurate description of the path toward isolation, self-centeredness, and loneliness in a person who is burdened
with sin. The ingathering of corporate worship leads to the unifica-
tion of persons who have a common experience of the forgiving
grace of God.

Thus the values of personal insight and social feeling are created,
conserved, and then multiplied in public worship. The radiation of
gratitude and self-acceptance lays the foundations upon which Christian worshipers can agree as to common goals and objectives for con-
certed Christian action. At this point, the work of a pastor, in the
secret places of personal counseling to change people's attitudes privately, becomes manifest in public work and social action as these
individuals set about righting glaring social wrongs in the community.

IV. Conclusion

The total task of the pastor presents an imposing responsibility.
Some ministers who read this description will feel that it is not in
keeping with the realistic problems of time and quantities of work
with which the average pastor must grapple. Such a concept of pastoral work in the context of the total function of the minister, however, implies radical departures in the underlying philosophy of
church administration.

American churches have been schematized according to two secular patterns of promotion: (1) mass production in business, which
depends upon volume rather than excellence of quality for profit,
and (2) promotional advertising techniques, which depend upon de-
personalized mediums of correspondence, telephone, and bulletins
for results. Churches and denominations have more or less unconsciously fallen into these same patterns by insisting upon the *largest*
congregations possible and relying upon cleverest techniques of
propaganda possible for the recruitment of members. All this moves
preaching and the sacraments to the center of the church life, and

insulates the pastor from personal contact with people, making of him an executive and administrator of a corporation rather than a shepherd of a flock.

The end result of this has been that the usefulness of the individual church member has decreased in direct proportion to the increase in the size of the congregation. He accepts less and less personal responsibility for the work of the Kingdom of God, and shifts more and more of it to paid workers. He gives less and less money to the causes of the Church, and the paid workers must depend more and more upon small gifts from the largest numbers of people. The early churches were in a reversed position. They were exclusive rather than inclusive in their membership. They emphasized personal rather than promotional values. They exerted influence and gave gifts all out of proportion to their numbers and wealth, because they " first . . . gave themselves."

The shift of philosophy to a rediscovery of the " face-to-face relationships " of the Christian *koinonia* calls, therefore, for four important changes. First, the pastoral care and personal counseling of individuals in an " open-faced " honesty between pastor and parishioners must become the heart of his work. His concern for *persons* as individuals in groups related to each other through families is the center of his personal values. All other functions of the pastor have meaning in terms of this concern for persons, and the use of his time and energy is gauged by it. Secondly, careful attention should be paid to the standards for admitting a person to the church, and the *active* membership of a church should be the *actual* membership. Heretofore, the standards of New Testament church life have been forgotten in the competitive bid for more and more " joiners." Careful preparation and personal counseling of new members in a church will result in fewer but stronger members. Indiscriminate herding of large numbers of people into a church does violence both to the personalities of the individuals involved and to the body of the church itself. Thirdly, this calls for smaller churches in order that one pastor, with adequate secretarial help, can be cared for himself and be left free to do the work of a true shepherd to a flock. The needs of a congregation of over five hundred people cannot be met adequately by one pastor. The great metropolitan churches are naturally forced to use several pastors who serve different functions. However, these are second-best substitutes for the relationship of one minister to one congregation of people who know each other personally. Nor are these the average, but the exceptional, churches.

Finally, these conclusions all imply that the church must have an aggressive missionary strategy for its own community. New churches must be formed in order to localize and personalize the ministry of both the pastor and the churches themselves. Individual churches cannot live on a competitive basis in relation to each other, therefore, but must devise plans for a co-operative missionary strategy in which the total life of the community as a whole is the primary concern of each group. This implies a co-operative rather than an organic relationship, in order that the autonomy of each face-to-face group may be conserved. At the same time the effectiveness of the social outreach of the whole Christian community can be increased.

PART TWO

PASTORAL METHODS

Chapter V

UNSPOKEN INFLUENCES ON PASTORAL METHODS

EVER since David rejected Saul's armor and chose to use his own slingshot, shepherds have been faced with the necessity of devising ways of working which are best adapted to their own personalities and the conditions under which they must function. Some methods of pastoral care, such as the minister's use of creative listening, are applicable to more situations than others. But no single technique or ideology is applicable to *all* the situations with which a minister has to deal.

Every relationship of a pastor to people is determined by many unspoken factors which tend unconsciously to be taken for granted by both the pastor and the person in need. But the success or failure of the relationship depends upon the pastor's ability to observe these influences and to take advantage of them as he chooses his methods of procedure. He should not remain unaware of them.

I. The Christian Equation

The religious situation of the person who comes to a pastor is the primary determinant of the methods which the pastor uses in his pastoral procedure. This is not to say that the basic problems of Christians are materially different from those of non-Christians, but rather it is to say that the spiritual resources available for the solution of such difficulties are different. The person who believes in God in Christ, who accepts as dependable and true the precepts of the Bible, and who has access to the friendship of the church is vastly richer than the person who does not have these bases of security.

Furthermore, this is not to say that the Christian pastor should have *one stereotyped* approach which he uses with non-Christians and

one other approach which he uses with members of his own flock —
making him a total of two procedures. Rather, it is to say that in non-
Christians a pastor confronts not only the necessity of discovering
the person's difficulty, but also that of introducing him to the resources of faith in Christ and the practice of His way. In the case
of a person who has Christian training and experience, the pastor
may draw upon that, although he may face the necessity of correct-
ing misinformation concerning Christian experience.

In both instances, however, the basic problem may be the same.
For instance, a thirty-year-old woman says that she can no longer
get any joy and security out of her prayer life, and feels that she may
have "backslidden." Another woman of approximately the same
age says that she has tried everything in order to find happiness with
her husband, and she has decided that the reason her home is not
happy is that she is not a Christian and does not have a safe place
on the inside of her heart. Both women, when careful exploration
of their difficulties is made, are found to be suffering from a sense of
sin over marital infidelities. In the case of the Christian, however,
the practice of Christian life is being hindered, and in the case of
the non-Christian the beginning of Christian experience is being
sought. Likewise, both women express deep feelings of insecurity
in their family as well as their religious relationships by reason of the
fact that both of them were neglected by their fathers as children
and by their husbands as adults. They were the children of inadequate fathers and are the wives of incompetent husbands. In both
instances, the basic difficulties are very similar, but the pastoral approach is quite different in each case because the religious attitudes
of the persons involved give a different structure to the basic difficulty.

II. The Nature of the Approach

Another determinant of pastoral technique is whether the person
came to the pastor of his own accord or had to be approached by the
pastor. Most pastors have had members of a person's family say to
them, "I want you to go talk to my husband, my wife, my brother,
my son, my daughter." Quite often this request comes just before

or just after a church gathering when little time is available. This is an opportunity to make an appointment with the person who makes the request. At this time the minister may say, " We can get a better picture of the situation then." Such an interview will often reveal the deeper motives the person has for wanting a minister to see the relative. It will cut down the possibilities of the minister's becoming a shield in the hands of one member of a family quarrel and a target for the other member.

Many people come to the pastor because of the insistence of someone whose approval they want very badly. For instance, a young girl may call for an appointment to talk over some premarital difficulties she is having with her boy friend. Upon arrival she says that she was reluctant to come herself, but her fiancé " twisted " her arm to get her to come to see the pastor. The necessity of gradually developing the consultation into one in which she herself wishes to participate rests upon the pastor. It may be that if she learns to make her own choices rather than let someone else do so, she has gone a long way toward preparing for a more stable marriage.

Ideally constructed, however, are those situations in which a person comes voluntarily, and not out of constraint, to his pastor about his own problems and not someone else's difficulty. Such a person has already spiritually prepared himself for the pastor's work. Even here, nevertheless, the minister must needs be sensitive to the person who is a chronic " counsel seeker," with the habit of going to first one person and then another without following through with his relationship to any of them. In listening to a person, the pastor will note the other pastor, teachers, doctors, psychiatrists, etc., to whom the person has been with his problem. If such information is not reflected by the person's own discussion, a pastor can tactfully ask for it at an opportune moment. If the person is not a member of a pastor's own congregation, a minister would do well to discover how it came to pass that this person chose to come to him. Such measures do much on the first interview to define one's relationship and to indicate the particular approach the pastor should follow and the technique he should use.

III. The Social Role of the Pastor

Gardner Murphy suggests that the social task or function carried out by an individual in a community is determined by the social role which the community assigns to him by virtue of the confidence it has in him as a person. This social role is made up, in our society, of the age status, the marital-sexual status, and the unique and individual features of the person who is called upon to perform a given task. All these combine to give a person his concept of himself and to give him status in the community that makes it possible for him to do his task more effectively. In a word, the pastor's concept of himself and the part that he is assigned in the drama of interpersonal relationships in his community largely determines the techniques with which he functions as a pastor.[17]

The pastor's age has an important bearing upon his methodology. The more nearly he is the same age of the person whom he seeks to help, the more of a fellowship approach he uses and the less social distance he has in the relationship. If he is much younger — or even if he is youthful only in appearance — older persons tend to mother him or father him. If he is middle-aged or elderly, young persons more readily express feelings of a filial nature. Inexperience enters to judge the young man and too much age causes some people to feel that the elderly man will not understand. The importance of the age relationship of a pastor to his parishioner is suggested in the advice of Paul to Timothy: " Do not rebuke an older man but exhort him as you would a father; treat younger men like brothers, older women like mothers, younger women like sisters, in all purity " (I Tim. 5:1, 2).

Then, too, the marital status of a pastor conditions his approach and method. Especially is this true in family counseling situations. A married pastor visiting a woman patient in a hospital finds her a great deal more at ease in speaking of the effect that her recent operation may have on her childbearing ability than would a single minister. Likewise, a married pastor who is also a parent would find

---

[17] Gardner Murphy, *Personality; a Biosocial Approach to Origins and Structure,* pp. 784 ff. Harper & Brothers, publishers, 1947.

more ease in this situation than would the pastor who has no children. Furthermore, single persons seem to feel more secure in giving confidences to a married minister. In such instances, women feel more secure because the married minister is not a potential husband. It seems that the pastoral situation calls either for a married man — with children, if possible — in the case of Protestant ministers, or for a celibate, as in the case of Catholic priests.

The New Testament calls for another trait, which is a subtle determinant of a pastor's methods. It requires that he be " given to hospitality." Another way of saying this is that the pastor is a " lover of strangers." The pastor's effectiveness as a counselor is determined by his ability to put those people at ease who are strangers to him and also to identify himself with people whose experience is quite often poles apart from his own. People of different standards, family background, social standing, education, and personal taste from his own nevertheless find it easy to identify with him. They feel that he loves them and welcomes them into his confidence. Such a pastor finds that all manner of people come to him with all manner of requests.

Of course, whether or not people turn to a pastor is largely determined by the personal magnetism of the man himself. All that has been said on the subject of the personal qualifications of the Christian shepherd is applicable here. The writers of the New Testament did not list such standards in order to be legalistic; they were searching for men to whom " the flock of God " could turn for personal counsel and spiritual edification. They were looking for the most spiritually healthy men they could find to be " physicians of the soul," men who did not themselves stand in need of a physician, and whose very shadow would have a healing effect.

IV. THE TIME ELEMENT

The time element conditions everything a pastor does. Face-to-face pastoral care of individuals is one of the most important things he does, but it is *only one of the numberless things he has to do*. The administrative responsibility of a complex organization, the social demands of his community life, and the constant pressure of his preaching ministry draw upon his time. Likewise, in most of the church bodies that have a congregational form of church government, the pastor has to discharge heavy responsibilities on governing boards of trustees and commissions. Special committees often take weeks of his time.

The result of these pressures has been that responsible pastors tend to fret under four great frustrations: (1) they do not have time to study, (2) they do not have time for their own families, (3) they do not have time for a face-to-face ministry to their people, and (4) they do not have time for the cultivation of their inner spirits before God. The pastor becomes an isolated, lonely, tired individual who is cut off from the fulfillment of the four basic functions in society that offer him personal satisfaction in fulfilling his call to service.

Therefore, the minister must take intelligent measures as to the use of his time. He needs to decide for himself what is important in the ministry and leave other things to persons who consider them important. Chang Ch'ao says, " Only those who take leisurely what the people of the world are busy about can be busy about what the people of the world are leisurely about."

The average minister loses a great deal of motion in his work because he does not *plan* the use of his time. One way of using one's time wisely is to keep an appointment book and to deal with more serious personal problems at a later time than when the person first presents them, excepting those cases of an acute emergency. For instance, a thirty-nine-year-old woman comes saying that her sixteen-year-old daughter has fallen in love with a twenty-six-year-old divorced man and plans to be married three months from now. The minister has preached three times and conducted a funeral that day. It is now eight forty-five in the evening. It would be wiser to make an appointment for one day during the week than to attempt to deal at length with the situation that night.

Another timesaving device is to break a personal conference into two or three forty-five-minute discussions rather than to spend three hours with a person all at once. Especially is this true when the situation is a chronic trouble of long standing and will hold for another week or two. Quite often ministers tell of having talked until three or four o'clock in the morning with people who come to them. Rarely does an interview of over an hour and a half in length accomplish anything constructive that was not achieved in the first hour. When the pastor breaks the interview into two or three conferences, he is worth three or four times as much to the person as if he used it all at once. The "fallowing" of the mind of the person enriches his understanding of himself; often he will *come to many of the same conclusions of his own accord* that the pastor would have *to tell* him in only one interview. This is not to say, however, that there will not be times when only one conference will be possible — such as those times when a pastor is the conference speaker at a religious assembly, and many other such occasions. Therefore, he must be continually studying ways and means of making one interview count for the most.

The *amount of available time* a minister has at his disposal in dealing with a person determines the techniques of counseling he uses in a given situation, the extent to which he can help the person himself, and the possible necessity of calling upon some other skilled and devoted worker to minister to the person along with him.

V. The Social Setting

Another atmospheric pressure on pastoral practice is *the social setting within which a man functions as a Christian shepherd*. Some social situations within which Christian ministers operate are *controlled* and some are *uncontrolled*. For instance, a chaplain in the Army, in addition to being a minister, is an officer. He is not financially dependent on the personnel who come to him for counsel, but rather their future can be changed by his intervention. The pastor of a congregation is dependent upon the persons with whom he counsels for his living and for his status as a minister. Another comparison is similar: a chaplain in a state hospital is not in danger of slander if some female patient, in transferring feelings to him, falls in love with him or accuses him of having made immodest sexual advances toward her, or if some male patient accuses him of a homosexual attack. But if a pastor in a small community has one such thing occur, his community position may be threatened. The Army and the hospital are *controlled social settings* and a church community is an *uncontrolled* social setting.

Then, again, Christian ministers function in *authoritarian* social settings and *permissive* environments. A chaplain in a prison or a delinquency reform school quite often represents the mind of the law to a prisoner or an adolescent child. A minister who teaches in a Church-related school has mixed roles of authority and permissiveness that often stalemate each other. The man who goes as pastor to a church where his predecessor was a " dictator of the people " inherits an authoritarian setting, and his people expect him also to tell them what to do so they can tell him where to go — too!

Again, it makes a vast difference whether the social setting of a pastor's counseling ministry is *rural* or *urban*. The majority of ministers work in a rural setting, i.e., in towns and villages of less than 2,500 population or in the open country. The rural minister spends most of his time in face-to-face relationships. Nevertheless, they are so informal, privacy is so difficult to achieve, and gossip and idle speculation are so active that he finds himself pressed in his attempts to meet his people's intimate and personal needs. Most of the literature on pastoral care and personal counseling helps him very little because few of the authors seem to have been in his situation. But some profound personality changes have been effected as a pastor sat with a fellow Christian on a woodpile after an " all day preaching and dinner on the ground," or as he sat fishing with one of the country doctors.

The rural minister also has fewer community agencies upon which to call and fewer competent specialists in the field of medicine with whom to work. This writer was lecturing to a group of rural ministers who told him that there was not a psychiatrist within a two-hundred-mile radius. Much that would be turned to other professional workers in a city must be carried along by the rural minister as best he can. The available resources for referral determine largely the pastoral techniques of a minister. A city pastor, in talking with a young mother of two children, finds that she cannot talk for crying about the hungry children at home whose father is mentally unbalanced and incompetent to support them. His situation is different here from that of a rural pastor. The city pastor calls the family service organization, which his church helps to support, and gets supervised economic assistance for the family and psychiatric help for the father. In the meantime, he comforts the mother with a spiritual ministry of prayer. Some of the other church women care for the children while the mother visits the husband in the hospital. The minister keeps in touch with the doctor as to how the church can meet the husband's needs. Both the husband and the psychiatrist are members of the minister's church.

The rural minister would be able to accomplish many of the same results but his procedure would be very difficult. In the first place, he could not call a family service organization because there might be no phone and no community chest. In the second place, he could not call a psychiatrist since there might be none within two hundred miles. He must turn to the state hospital, and he knows that the patient may receive inadequate institutional care and no psychiatric treatment at all. So, instead, the minister turns to the neighbors, and in loving tenderness the men gather in the patient's crop and the women see to it that the family is fed. The pastor in the meantime takes the mother and father to a nearby city to a great clinic where treatment for the father is available.

VI. The Age Level

The age level of those who come to a pastor also determines his method of dealing with them. A child below the age of ten usually presents his fears and worries in the form of action and behavior rather than verbal descriptions. Of course, this is no monopoly of little children, but is also characteristic of immature adults. But little children usually embody their problems in the stories they tell and the games they play. Extremely old people quite often need companionship and reassurance in a bereavement whereas a twenty-eight-year-old man whose wife died suddenly needs an additional and different type of ministry. The developmental process of aging needs careful study by a minister as he seeks to adapt the eternal truth of the gospel to the changing situations of little children, young lovers, young parents, middle-aged people, retiring and declining people, and senile folk. *Emotional Problems of Living,* by O. S. English and G. H. J. Pearson, is a readable book which describes the growth of personality.

VII. LEVEL OF INTELLIGENCE

Most pastors have no specific way of knowing the basic level of intelligence of their people. Close attention to muscular skills and co-ordination, extent and use of vocabulary, extent of education, the repetition of grades at any point along the way, and reasons for dropping out of school are all ways of making a rough guess. Suffice it to say that the lower the level of intelligence, the less good use can be made of verbal discussions and the more nearly one has to treat a person as he would a child.

The point at which extreme cases of low intelligence come to the attention of a pastor is in his home visitation. For instance, a pastor heard of a rural family of three children in which the second child was, as they put it, " afflicted." A brief home visit was made during which the child screamed and beat his mother in the face, jumped up in the pastor's lap and tried to bite him, and caused his brothers and sisters also considerable discomfort. Finally, the children ran out to play, at which time the mother expressed her great distress over the " afflicted " child. She asked for her pastor's guidance and the way was made clear for the pastor to say: " You feel that the child, however much you love him, is getting in the way of the other children's normal growth? Have you ever thought of placing him in an institution? " This question led easily to the referral of the mother to a nearby child-guidance clinic where she found institutional care for the child.

The father of another feeble-minded child presented this problem on a fishing trip with his pastor: " I was a mighty mean man before I became a Christian. Do you feel like God may have given this dull child to me to punish me for my sins?" The pastor countered with a question: "How do you think that would make the child feel toward God?"

VIII. The Family Situation

Such an illustration indicates that the family situation of a person is an all-important determinant of a pastor's method of dealing with him. It is a fact that "the individual tends to relive his primary family group experience in any group to which he belongs." For instance, in the academic atmosphere, the major professor becomes a parent substitute, the associate professor becomes a rival brother, and the student in conflict with both of them may turn to the college pastor for arbitration of disputes much as he did to his mother as a child. This concept is aptly portrayed in Wittenberg's book, *So You Want to Help People*. The dynamic factors in pastoral situations thus arise from a habit-formed pattern of family relationships. These in turn condition the technique to be used in relation to individuals.

IX. The Cultural Pattern

Another determining factor in the use of pastoral techniques is the cultural pattern of the various people with whom the pastor works. What is very funny and would increase friendship and rapport in one culture would be the occasion of a fight in another culture. The pattern of social inferiority, hypersensitivity to criticism, and embarrassment over family background characteristic of the Southern cotton mill student who "goes off to college" determines even the exact phraseology of a pastor's interview with him. A person from an upper social level quite often would be conscience-stricken over having done a thing that a person from a lower social level would not give a second thought, and vice versa.[18]

[18] This is one of the valuable conclusions reached by Kinsey in the survey of sexual behavior of the human male in America. Also, J. S. Plant, *Personality and the Cultural Pattern,* Commonwealth Fund, 1937, and Liston Pope, *Millhands and Preachers,* Yale University Press, 1942, give detailed analyses of this determinant.

Especially is this true of social practices that are sanctioned or tabooed by the community in which a pastor works. The minister needs enough social insight to locate the dangers that caused the taboos, and enough social feeling to walk circumspectly among his people.

Accordingly, the degree of prestige of a minister varies from one cultural group to another. Having worked in the Elgin State Hospital in Illinois and the Kentucky State Hospital in Kentucky, this writer discovered that, as a minister, his role as " the preacher " was accepted and even respected with awe by the Kentucky patients, whereas the second-generation Europeans at Elgin hardly distinguished him from any other type of worker. The cultural pattern of the person with whom the pastor counsels determines the level on which he can be approached and the method that the pastor uses. Therefore, one's pastoral role is conditioned by his whereabouts, and the pastor must be as versatile in his approaches to different cultural groups as was Paul in dealing with people of such vast cultural differences as existed between the Galatians and the Corinthians.

X. Physical and Mental Health

A minister is required by the nature of his calling to visit the sick. Much of his time will be spent in the company of physically and mentally ill people. Dealing with such persons calls for a radical shift of method as compared with people who are physically sound, clothed, and in their right mind.

This requires that the Christian pastor be a close ally of the medical experts who also minister to his people. Many of the problems that people present to a minister have an organic cause, and the minister often does a service when he tactfully suggests a complete physical checkup. Fortunate indeed is the pastor if the physician to whom he refers a person is a Christian who has had psychiatric training in his medical education. Only the younger physicians have had such training, as a general rule, but it is necessary if a doctor is to have a total view of the patient as a person.

Furthermore, the minister himself needs enough psychiatric information to be able to detect incipient mental disorders and to know when to seek medical help in his ministry to his people.[19] This is not to say that he is to usurp the function of a doctor, nor is it to say that he will forsake the simplicities of the " language of Zion " for the technical terms of another field of study. It does mean, however, that he needs the capacity and proper information with which to " try the spirits " which take hold of his people, to see whether they are of God or not.

The pastor can ordinarily suspect deep-seated mental pathologies when the person who comes to him is deluded with exceptionally *grandiose, unrealistic,* and *detailed* plans for his own redemption or destruction of the world. An example is a twenty-seven-year-old girl who went to the Wednesday prayer service and made a dedication of her life to Christian service. Afterward she told her pastor that the Holy Spirit was driving her to ask *everyone* if he were a Christian. Consequently, she did not sleep, eat, or rest for over a week; rather, at all hours of the night she would go to the homes of people whom she did not know and ask them if they were Christians. Her pastor quickly discerned the situation, and helped the family to secure psychiatric aid. The girl was hospitalized, restored to her mental balance, and returned to her work as a librarian within ten weeks. The careful attention and devotion of her pastor detected her condition early and the good results were partially due to the pastor's soundness of judgment.

Again, a person may become deluded with overwrought *feelings of persecution,* as did a woman who felt that her God was trying to make her leave her husband and children to become a prophetess who would marry the savior of the world. Anyone who sought to help her was a " frustrator of the grace of God."

[19] Clinical pastoral training in a mental hospital is designed to give this kind of equipment to the pastor. Firsthand experience under supervision has no substitute. However, reading such books as follow will help considerably:

Karl Menninger, *The Human Mind,* Third Edition. Alfred A. Knopf, Inc., 1947.

George Preston, *The Substance of Mental Health.* Rinehart & Co., Inc., 1943.

D. K. Henderson and R. D. Gillespie, *A Text-Book of Psychiatry for Students and Practitioners,* Sixth Edition. Oxford University Press, 1947.

Then, too, the person who is profoundly and unexplainably *depressed* may be suspected of being mentally ill. This means that the person's melancholia is unreasonable or is concerned with some triviality. An example is the case of a woman who wept profusely and continually over having caught the wrong bus when she went shopping. Often deep depressions come to the pastor's attention in those persons who are convinced that the " Holy Spirit has left them," and that they have committed " the unpardonable sin." They are usually quite vague and abstract as to specific things they have done.

Depressed persons may be *agitated* and hand-wringing, *perplexed* and confused, *stuporous* and unable to talk at all, or *philosophical* and questioning. *No amount* of reassurance comforts them, and *no reasoning* convinces them that God cares and is able to forgive them.

Any pastor can readily see that among these various types of depressed persons, no *one* approach is applicable to all situations. As Dr. E. E. Landis, chief of the Norton Psychiatric Service, has said, " A person can use a listening catharsis approach in relation to some depressed people and he may precipitate a suicide! "

Such is one of the dangers of a minister's attempting to deal with psychiatric patients without the help of a specialist, and in an uncontrolled environment. One of the easiest ways of answering one's own questions concerning the mental health of a person is to determine whether or not the person is *dangerous to himself and to other people.* The threat of suicide or homicide, the disturbance of the peace of others by becoming a public nuisance, and the loss of the capacity for supporting one's self are the social results of mental illness that indicate institutional care for the person. This is ordinarily a complicated legal procedure, varying from state to state, with which a pastor should acquaint himself thoroughly. Only the family of a person can be responsible for instituting such procedure, and a pastor should *never* assume this responsibility himself.

These are the more obvious symptoms of mental illness; the more subtle ones take closer and more skilled attention. The first place where such illnesses manifest themselves is *in disturbances of the family and work routine of a person.* He may cease to eat, stay up all night for no apparent cause, leave his work without explanation, or fail to remember when he is on duty. An example is the man who quit his work in an automobile plant, went back to the community in which he grew up and had left many years before, registered in the hotel, but would not go to his parents' home. He did not eat, sleep, or leave the room and barricaded the door against all visitors.

Then, again, *unusual changes in personal grooming* suggest mental illness. A beautiful and dainty woman who has in the past been known for her immaculateness of appearance comes to her pastor's study. He observes fresh food stains on her blouse, disheveled hair, misplaced lipstick, and dirty fingernails. Likewise, *misplaced remarks and acts,* inappropriate emotions and behavior suggest mental illness. For instance, a young mother meets her pastor on Monday morning and accuses him of having tried to kill her children. Such behavior calls for an exceptional kind of pastoral method. Therefore, a pastor would do well to gauge a person's relative degree of mental competence as an important determinant of all his counseling methods.

Finally, the forerunner of an open mental break is the observable increase in the *degree of compulsion* with which a person lives and does his deeds. When in the major portion of a person's life he is compelled to do things apart from his own choice and against his own better judgment — by constraint and not willingly — he is in the danger zone of mental safety.

These conditioning factors — the Christian equation, the personal desire for help, the social role of the pastor, the time element, the social setting, the age level, the intelligence level, the family situation, the cultural pattern, and physical and mental health — are unspoken influences in every situation in which a pastor works. His ability to observe silently these facts and to gauge his own methods according to what he sees and senses largely determines his success or failure as a pastor. In no sense of the word does an unfavorable condition at any one of these ten points relieve the pastor of all responsibility for the spiritual care of the person at hand. The responsibility may be all the heavier. The person is still " one for whom Christ died." The method, however, whereby the pastor tends the flock of God is modified considerably by these factors.

Chapter VI

THE LEVELS OF PASTORAL CARE

The Christian pastor cares for people on many different levels of relationship. At one and the same time, he may be the personal friend, next-door neighbor, pastor-preacher, pastor-counselor, and golf or fishing companion of the person to whom he ministers. Furthermore, he does not, unless he is a pastor in an unusually large city, spend much time with people whom he never sees again after he has finished a series of three or four interviews. He is related to the same persons over a period of years, during which his relationship moves from one level to another and back again, depending upon the variety of crises endured.

These are the facts that make it unwise for pastors to carry over *in toto* the office techniques of professional counselors of any kind, or of dubbing their work as " pastoral psychiatry," to use Bonnell's phrase. It is true that hospital chaplains, professors of pastoral psychology in seminaries, a few " specialist " pastors such as John S. Bonnell, Norman Vincent Peale, and others have a good deal of very formal counseling to do. A few exceptionally large churches have placed clinically trained pastors on their staffs to do nothing but such formal counseling of people who are referred to them. Every pastor needs to know what to do when he is called upon for " deeper level " pastoral care which might be characterized as " nonmedical forms of psychotherapy." But the fact remains that specialized and controlled situations are the exception rather than the rule in the pastorate. Therefore, the average minister cannot depend on the methods of a specialist unless he has the necessary training for such work and the same controlled conditions under which to work.

Rather, the pastor does best to study and to evaluate the specific level on which he does have access to the personal confidence of people to whom he is related in a helpful way. On that level he can begin work where he finds himself. He must be flexible enough to adapt himself to a person on *that level of relationship at which he can best serve him*. When the pastor does this, he discovers several different levels on which an individual reacts to him as another human being to whom he can reveal himself. He will also find different levels of the individual's personal insight into his own problems and willingness to do something about them before God.

These areas of action may be called *the levels of pastoral care*. Another way of describing them would be to call these levels *types of pastoral care*. Preference is given to calling them levels for two reasons: First, these levels tend to appear in any given relationship of pastoral care in the order in which they are to be described in the following pages. Therefore, the character of a relationship may change perceptibly within the scope of a single hour, or from one conference to another with the same person. Secondly, the depth psychologists have been sufficiently convincing that a pastor needs to learn from them. A knowledge of the deeper layers of personality reveals that the most important forces that determine behavior are quite often unconscious to the clear level of awareness of a person. In the pastoral relationship, as it grows with time and acquaintance, " deep calleth unto deep," and " in the hidden part " people are made to know wisdom. Thus the pastoral bond is more than a mere " telling " of things by one person to another. It is the provocation of wisdom through an especial relationship. This is essentially a Hebrew concept in which a distinction is drawn between the Hebrew word which means " to tell " in the sense one would learn from reading a book, and another which means " to cause to know," in the sense in which one learns by immediate, firsthand experience. It is something of what the men of the Samaritan village meant when they said, " It is no longer because of your words that we believe, for we have heard for ourselves, and we know that this is indeed the Savior of the world " (John 4:42).

Christian experience, when seen from the vantage point of levels of feeling relationships, moves from hearsay *about* Christ to the level of personal acquaintance *with* Christ and personal dependence *upon* Christ, to the level of learning *from* Christ, to the level of confession *to* Christ, to the level of healing *by* Christ to the level of reconciliation *with* Christ, and finally achieves spiritual usefulness on the level of comradeship *alongside* Christ to witness *for* Christ.

The minister as an " ambassador for Christ " by his own spiritual maturity must have reached the level of comradeship with and witness for Christ. As he does this and people seek his personal counsel by reason of his accurate representation of Christ, he works " on behalf of Christ." Then, he works in accord with the example of Christ and the nature of Christian experience on *five different levels of pastoral care* of people in terms of their movement toward spiritual maturity. These levels are: the level of friendship, the level of comfort, the level of confession, the level of teaching, the level of counseling and psychotherapy. On every level he is a witness to the good news of the grace of God in Christ. His ultimate objective is the development of a co-worker in the Kingdom of God.

I. The Level of Friendship

The Protestant pastor most aptly comes to his people in the role of a friend. The term " brother," by which many church people call their minister, reflects the democratic friendship they have for one who is " first among equals." The pastor mingles as a friend and neighbor with the people whom he serves. He goes to wedding gatherings, all-day meetings, young people's social gatherings, and many kinds of men's social clubs. His being " given to hospitality " is an asset to him. It is soon sensed, if he is hard to get to know and does not mingle well with people.

On social occasions, timid, isolated, and withdrawn persons can come to know their minister, and their confidence in him can be so established that they will later say, " It was at the ' 4-H ' cattle show when you stopped and said hello that I decided that, if I ever got courage to tell this to anybody, you would be the kind of person I could talk with." This establishment of rapport is the gracious making of oneself accessible to people, and not the compulsive falling over oneself to " win friends and influence people." This latter attitude springs more from the fear of not being approved by others than it does from an easy sense of affection for people for their own sakes.

The ministry of friendship is the indispensable necessity of all other deeper levels of pastoral work. It is the seedbed of any fruitful service to people. Furthermore, a great majority of the real help that comes to people in crises is through persons whom they would term "just a good friend," and not through professional people or "full-time Christian workers." Some of the most effective pastoral care in churches has been done by lay persons who have had rich experience as parents and who are masters at the simple business of making, meriting, and keeping friends, i.e., they are "given to hospitality." Ways of teaching this rudiment of the Christian life should be devised in the educational program of the church.

The establishment of a friendly confidence with a person who comes for help needs, however, to be objective, and unencumbered by too much reference to mutual acquaintances and to the personal life of the pastor. For instance, a pastor was visited by a member of a nearby church. When he made a friendly reference to the pastor of that church, the woman became somewhat restless. The pastor, sensing her uneasiness, found it necessary to say, " But, of course, you know that when people come to me for a special kind of confidential help I do not talk over their problems in any way with anyone else except at their request or with their permission."

The ministry of friendship and example is the extent of a pastor's ministry to many people. It is the main necessity in his relationship to people of other denominations. In hospital visitation, a minister finds this " social approach " of a " hello visit " with Catholic and Jewish patients, and to persons who are the responsibility of another Protestant minister, most valuable. Likewise, the ministry of friendship to small children is exceptionally rewarding. Pastors give little children an example, a hero with whom to identify, and a friendship that lends security. Especially is this true in instances in which the home has been broken by death or separation of parents.

Whereas the objective, considerate management of a personal friendship is one of the least artificial and most effective means of changing human character at the pastor's disposal, naturally it has severe limitations. Many pastors complain that their people think of them as a " hail fellow well met," but seem to avoid situations in which a private, serious conversation about the deeper issues of life can be discussed. An example of this is the rural pastor who is always greeted by a large gathering of neighbors when he goes to take a meal at the home of his parishioners. The host and hostess feel the need for their neighbors' presence also in "entertaining" the preacher. Whereas this may turn out to be an excellent opportunity for an informal kind of *group* guidance, it does not allow much room for personal conference with an individual or for intimate acquaintance with a family group.

Again, the pastor may find himself socially identified with his people in such a way that the amount of social distance necessary for them to reach out for his care and help will be lost. Familiarity need not breed contempt, but it does represent a loss of effectiveness in a pastor's leadership when he becomes just "another one of the boys" and his "separateness" as a man of God is completely obscured by his "togetherness" with the people of the community.

This suggests the most outstanding limitation of the social level of a pastor's ministry: there are some things a person can tell only to a stranger. As one person said in conference with a pastor in a neighboring community: " I would not dare tell these things to my own pastor because he knows all the people I do. I have no doubt that he would never tell a soul. I have confidence in him, but I feel that I must talk to someone who is not so close to me." Certainly a pastor needs to be able to " entertain strangers."

But in spite of such limitation, the pastor's friendly access to people in the natural setting of their homes is his greatest opportunity for careful observation of their personal needs and for a " saltlike " influence on their behavior.

II. THE LEVEL OF COMFORT

The pastor at his best, like Jesus, is thought of as "a man of sorrows, and acquainted with grief." Under inevitable hardships, people turn to their pastor for spiritual fortification, emotional support, and affectionate companionship. Here the Christian shepherd goes with his people into the " valley of the shadow of death," stands beside them in the testing times of great tragedies such as economic failures, intolerable losses of self-respect, and terrors of such calamities as war, flood, pestilence, and economic depression. People of every walk of life traditionally give the minister this task in life, and expect him to fulfill a ministry of encouragement and comfort. " If he is not available when people are in trouble," said one layman, " a minister need not be on hand any other time."

The different situations in which a ministry of comfort is needed are legion. *Bereaved persons* most often are in need of the supporting help of a minister. Those who are facing death lean heavily upon their pastors, and draw upon the sources of spiritual strength which he has to offer and which he represents. Likewise, the minister's approach to *persons with long-term chronic illnesses* such as tuberculosis, the more serious kinds of arthritis, and the many afflictions of old age, is usually one of companionate encouragement. A supportive ministry is also a necessity in the case of *persons who are permanently handicapped,* such as blind persons, persons who have lost a limb, or those who have been paralyzed. Such losses are much like the loss of a loved person by death, and the process of mourning over the loss through which these persons go, in adjusting to their plight, is much the same process through which a bereaved person goes. Closely akin to bereavement is the plight of parents of deformed or mentally deficient children, who continually need fortification of spirit. In the same grouping of difficulties in which a supportive ministry of comfort is indicated are *those persons suffering from acute physical pain,* which often is so intense that painkilling drugs seem to be of little avail. The pain itself is aggravated by the straining tension with which the excited person fights to bear the suffering. The first step in relief is relaxation, which quite often comes through the efforts of a well-poised minister, who does not waver in the presence of trouble, who is relatively serene in the presence of fear.

Furthermore, *mentally depressed persons,* whose reasons for being depressed lie unrecognized in the unconscious, need a supportive ministry of comfort. Rational attempts at analyzing their troubles and giving them a ready-made solution quite often meet with failure, which in turn depresses such persons all the more. Most often they are in need of a medical doctor as well as a minister, although they quite regularly go to the minister first. The possibility of suicide in such cases is rather high, and caution should be taken at every move.

Another group of persons who vitally need the ministry of comfort that a pastor can afford are the *disappointed lovers* of his parish. A smile flits across most people's minds when such persons are mentioned, but a pastor cannot afford to let humor be his *only* treatment for persons who have been seriously hurt in a love affair. Efforts at "patching" up such situations usually are less valuable and more dangerous than a ministry of comfort and supportive encouragement of the person who expresses such a grief to his pastor.

More specifically, the "how" of a pastor's ministry of comfort consists of the oldest methods of personal influence that exist: *suggestion, catharsis,* and *reassurance.* These methods have fallen into the criticism of those who have often seen them used to exploit rather than to bless human life. Nevertheless, even the worst use of an instrument does not justify the condemnation of the means itself, but only of the ends toward which it is used.

The minister often underestimates the tremendous power of *suggestion,* which his presence itself carries in the lives of those who actively despise the way of life in which he walks. Paul expressed it accurately when he said that " we are the aroma of Christ to God among those who are being saved and among those who are perishing. . . . Who is sufficient for these things? " (II Cor. 2:15, 16). The pastor's presence itself is a spiritual fortification as he comes alongside people in time of stress and sits where they sit as a reminder of the presence of God.

The knowledge of this fact should relieve the minister of the compulsive necessity to "say something" on *every* occasion, because there are many times when silence itself is a means of prayer during those "groanings which cannot be uttered." Especially within the fellowship of the household of the Christian faith, among those who share a common loyalty to a living Christ, "there is no speech nor language, without these their voice is heard " (Ps. 19:3, marginal reading). Job aptly railed at his comforters: " Ye are all physicians of no value. Oh that ye would altogether hold your peace! And it would be your wisdom " (Job 13:4, 5). The minister today who has not learned the disciplined and re-creative use of silence as a means of spiritual communication falls into the same condemnation.

Not only is the minister's presence a spiritual fortification to his people, but his capacity to listen to their griefs affords a *catharsis* of the spirit for them. Catharsis is something more here than confession: it is a sharing of difficulty in which the weight of pain, grief, and disappointment is actually lightened. As Bacon has said, the sharing of a trouble cuts it in half, but the sharing of a joy doubles its strength. The observant minister finds that his people's expressions of deep feelings in times of bereavement afford him an unexcelled opportunity to co-operate with the Spirit of God in the growth of the soul through grief crises. He knows that at the earlier stages the bereaved person quite often *cannot* talk about the loved one, but at a later stage he *needs* to talk.

Such a catharsis also restores the perspective of the person and helps him to lay hold of the positive forces working in his behalf. Likewise, it gives him access to the pastor and the community resources, which the pastor represents. And in many instances, the pastor's actual supportive ministry will lie in the use of the Christian fellowship groups to " prop up " a weaker brother, or to support a " wounded comrade " rather than to engage in a minute analysis of an unchangeable situation.

Much of the pastor's time, also, will be given over to reassuring his people. *Reassurance* is a primary method of comfort, and is a necessary part of the pastoral ministry. A pastor says to a young college student who has an intolerable sense of inferiority because of the cultural backwardness of his family: " You are going to do an acceptable year of college work. I know you are, because your high school principal told me that you have good intelligence, and I have seen that you are willing to work." This is reassurance, and the pastor may find himself saying it more than once. A pastor may say to a forty-one-year-old woman who has just recently given birth to a child and feels that she is not " a fit mother " for him: " You have told me why you feel that you cannot go through with this. You have also told me that you would die if you had to give the baby up. You *can* carry through if you really *want* to do so; that I believe in you. I want to encourage you in your struggle to be a responsible parent." This is reassurance, and the woman may need to talk with the pastor again and again and receive such encouragement.

Naturally, the use of reassurance incurs many problems. First of all, the pastor should be careful that this encouragement of people is in keeping with the facts of their own situation, and not idle words said just to make them feel good. Idle encouragement given as a palliative does more harm than good. But a hardheaded optimism that nevertheless faces the facts makes of a minister one who imparts hope. A careless reassurance, on the other hand, can cause a person to feel that his pastor is minimizing his troubles and does not understand at all. Quite often this breaks the relationship completely and the person searches for help elsewhere.

Again, ministers readily become trite, impersonal, and vague in the reassurances they give people. Their encouragement is not based on *attention* to the personal problem of the individual to whom they are talking, *consideration* of the way in which the person will hear what they say, nor *care* for the essential well-being of the person and those other people to whom he is related. Therefore, ministers are likely to say the same things to everyone regardless of the specific nature of their trouble. For instance, a minister was talking to one of his most substantial contributors during an illness that called for hospitalization. At the age of forty-three this man was suffering from hypertension, arteriosclerosis, and a reactive depression. He was on the verge of a divorce from his wife for having carried on a clandestine love affair for ten years, and his business was facing failure. Not knowing these facts at all, his pastor visited him for about eight minutes, at the conclusion of which he said: " You are going through the deep waters. I have had all the troubles you are going through, and I can say to you from experience that if you will just put your trust in the Bible, you will come through."

Such an approach at best missed the mark of the man's need. This is not to say that the pastor's words were insincere; it is to say, however, that they were shots at random rather than being carefully aimed at the man's situation itself.

The resources of prayer and Scripture-reading are especially helpful in the ministry of comfort. The pastor brings the assurances of the power of God through prayer. Prayer therefore should be handled as carefully as any other powerful explosive would be handled. Several guides should indicate the use of prayer in any given situation: (1) The *appropriateness* of the atmosphere is one guide. To bring formal prayer into an atmosphere of frivolity or empty gossip often is to do violence to the nature of prayer. (2) Again, *brevity* is a guide to the use of formal prayer. This means that every word must count, and that words be chosen to fit the need of the person to whom the pastor is ministering. This rules out the use of trite, worn-out phrases which are used not only by liturgical ministers, but also by those who decry "form prayer." Spontaneity in prayer is to be desired, but this is not to say that the language of prayer is not a thing that can be learned. The best-written prayers are found in the Bible, and the language of the Bible is the language of prayer. The pastor does well to carry great sections of the Bible in his memory for use in his prayers (Ps. 1; 15; 23; 37; 46; 51; 79:8, 9; 90; 91; 103; 139; Isa. 40:28–31; Matt., ch. 6; John, ch. 14; Rom., ch. 8; I Cor., ch. 13; II Cor. 4:15–18; Eph. 3:14–21; *et al.*, are good examples of the "patience and comfort of the Scriptures").

(3) *Relaxation* is another principle of prayer. For this reason, prayer should never be used merely as an excuse to end a conference with a person. Often prayer will be the point at which a person moves from a social level of conversation to the deeper levels of concern. For example, a pastor was visiting a rural family in which the mother was seriously ill. After a brief conversation, the mother asked, as her custom was, that he read a passage of the Bible to her. This he did and led a brief prayer for God's strength to be afforded the sick woman and that the love of her family would be a medicine in itself. After the prayer, the pastor did not hurry to say good-by. Rather, he paused in silence a long while. Then the mother told him

of her fear that she was dying, and the pastor had an opportunity to minister to her personally as a comforting strength in her last few weeks of life. He could not have done this had he himself been tense, in a hurry, and devoid of relaxation.

(4) Finally, *prayer means more to a person if he voluntarily asks for it himself*. The pastor can do much to cause people to be at ease in asking for such a ministry. In many cases it is taken for granted that he will pray — such as in cases of acute illness, impending death, recent death, etc. But these are not the rule. The pastor can say, " There are many things a pastor can do for his people, and I wonder if there is anything that *I* can do for you? " The tone of voice inflects meaning, and the person may ask, as one woman did, " Well, I had never thought of that; what *are* the things ministers do for people? " Then the pastor had an opportunity to interpret his ministry of prayer to her. It was made easy for her to say she would like him to pray.

Likewise, the use of the Scriptures for purposes of reassurance, comfort, and support is especially valuable. Dr. John S. Bonnell demonstrates this especially well in his books. The use of the concise, easily remembered verses of the Scriptures, especially the winnowed wisdom of Psalms and Proverbs, provides an undergirding for the minds of people. Their effect increases with repetition and multiplies when they are memorized. The pastor does well to leave a passage with a person for later reading. A pastor may with profit prepare a set of chosen Scriptures for people with different types of difficulties, in a sort of " spiritual prescription."

III. THE LEVEL OF CONFESSION

A pastor visited one of his parishioners at her home inasmuch as she was the victim of an incurable cancer. She was thirty-nine years of age, the mother of two grown children by her first husband from whom she was divorced. At this time she was married to a second husband who had also been divorced previously. On his first visit, the pastor was received cordially and the woman told him how good the Lord had been to her, and how she had been given divine assurance that she would be healed. Then she asked the pastor to pray for her. His ministry was that of listening and prayer. Twice a week he visited the woman, and each time she protested almost too much that everything was all right between her and God. Finally, the necessity for skilled nursing help prompted the family to move her to the hospital.

At the hospital the pastor visited her regularly, and was met with the same overstated protestations of her assurances of God's care. The pastor listened with a sympathetic concern but without entering into the woman's conflicting feelings. One day, however, the woman said with great force that she was sure that she was a saved woman, and that God was going to help her get well. Then the pastor ventured a remark: "Then *everything* is all right between you and God, is it?" In a startled fashion, the woman said: "Have you been talking to somebody? Do you know something that is not right between me and God?" The pastor said, "I know nothing about you except what you yourself have told me." Then the sick woman clutched at her pastor's hand and fearfully asked him to pray for her. He prayed that she might understand herself in the light of God's love and discover the peace of God that passes understanding. After a long silence he left.

Four days later he returned. The woman was very sick and close to death. When he entered the room, the woman sent all her relatives away in order that she might talk in private with her pastor. Then she said: "I have sins in my life that I must talk about before I die. I have confessed them to God many times and each time he has told me to confess them before men. You are God's minister and I must tell you." Then she proceeded to reveal a crushing load of guilts connected with a series of acts that involved her close relatives and friends over a period of twenty-three years. In great remorse she sought the assurance of God's forgiveness. Then the pastor brought to her the "patience and comfort of the Scriptures" that assured her of God's healing redemption in Christ.

This is an example of the confessional ministry like those which every veteran minister could describe. This ministry has been institutionalized by the Catholics on a compulsory basis. By the law of reaction, Protestants have neglected the importance of confessing their "faults one to another." This is one of the first functions of the Christian community, and the restoration of those overtaken in faults is characteristic of Christians who have not become so sophisticated that they no longer feel the need for the confession of sin.

The fact remains that Protestant ministers, who are near to the heart of God and sensitive to the feelings of their people, still listen to the confessions of their people. A mother cries in bitter repentance for her mistakes in rearing her children. An otherwise respectable bank teller confesses a series of thefts for the first time to his pastor because he can no longer bear the guilt alone nor tolerate the fear of being caught. A young man confesses the paternity of an unborn child and seeks the aid of his pastor in protecting the mother and child. A young white woman has suddenly fallen in love with a Negro classmate in a great university and knows that her Southern parents will not understand. A husband confesses his marital infidelity and seeks to find its causes and remedy. A defense worker, caught by tuberculosis, confesses his money madness that caused him to work too many hours, too many days, and brought him to his bed.

The common characteristic of all these confessions is that they are all of a social nature involving many other people. But many confessions are more individualized, and the person condemns himself for the evil character of his private thought life. Or, he or she may confess the practice of masturbation, as did one fourteen-year-old boy who felt that he was mentally affected by melancholia for having indulged in this practice.

Several facts need to be considered in the practice of a confessional ministry. First, isolation is the main effect of a known transgression. The person cannot face his community as he did before. He is "cut . . . off from the land of the living" and from before the face of God. The confession is, therefore, more than a mere catharsis; it is also a socialization of an otherwise isolated experience. The person achieves a sense of togetherness with the people whose approval he considers most worth-while, as well as with the eternal God. As Washington Gladden has said, the load of shame and remorse can be removed if the pastor "can draw forth the rankling secret, and convince the troubled soul, *first by his own forgiveness,* that the Infinite Love is able to save to the uttermost all who trust in him." [20]

Again, the pastor must be careful in his ministry of confession not to accept too quickly the stated problem or the confessed sin as the real one. This could be called the " Aha reflex," in which a minister feels like saying, " Eureka! " when a person tells him of some foul deed. Especially is this true of confessions of sexual sins. These gross offenses are often merely the symptoms of deeper and more persistent ones. For instance, a young unmarried woman may confess the fact that she is with child, whereas her heaviest burden of guilt hovers around a burning hatred for her father who is the chairman of the official board of the church. Her act is an expression of her hatred of her father and an inadvertent way of bringing shame upon him.

Another hazard to avoid in the confessional ministry is to take the admission of a fault too lightly and to reassure the person to the point that he is made to feel guilty over having felt guilty. This is most common in one's ministry to children and adolescents. An adolescent boy or girl may be having all manner of difficulty over some seemingly insignificant habit. The pastor may pass the whole thing off so lightly — even with humor — and miss the deep feelings the person has about his behavior. This applies not only to adolescents but also to adults. For instance, a thirty-five-year-old woman, upon being asked by her pastor if she had been to church recently, said, " No, I do not feel comfortable when I'm sitting in church." When pressed unduly for a reason, she said with great embarrassment, " I constantly fear that someone will hear my insides growl out loud." A touch of humor eased her tension. Then the pastor said: " I know that is not completely funny to you; I want you to know that I take it seriously. Would you like to talk with me more about these fears sometime? Maybe I can help you." This conversation led easily to another and the woman confessed great remorse over having had an abortion performed several years before. She greatly desired children at that time and could not have them. There was a direct connection between her fear of her " insides being noticed "

[20] *Op. cit.,* p. 86. Italics mine.

in church and her guilt over this deed.

The ministry of confession is closely related to medical psychotherapy, but *there is a vital difference.* The woman to whom reference has just been made was referred to her pastor by a psychiatrist. He stated the difference this way: " Here was a woman suffering from a sense of sin about wrong deeds she had actually committed. She needed forgiveness from God, and there was very little need of my trying to turn theologian. I referred her to her pastor. Now the people a psychiatrist can help are those who are *deluded* and *think* they have committed crimes of which they are innocent, or who are hearing voices telling them that the room is electrically wired in such a way as to cause them to murder."

The confessional ministry calls for different methods of approach according to the age of the person involved and the degree of " full-grownness " of the sins the person confesses. A child needs information and guidance in the presence of ignorance, temptation, and sin. An unwitting error cannot be treated in the same way a highhanded and premeditated crime is treated. Great care must be taken in distinguishing a temptation from a sin, because many people experience more guilt over the things they are tempted to do than they do over the sins they actually commit. Likewise, many people are afflicted with diseases that cause them to do things against their own good judgment and they are powerless to control their actions. In such cases, it is the minister's task to heal the volition and strengthen the person's sense of personal responsibility rather than to add to his loneliness and desperation by losing patience with him. Quite often such persons as epileptics, acute alcoholics, sex perverts, and psychopathic thieves and liars are in need of a physician as well as a minister, because they are afflicted with diseases that express their symptoms in the moral behavior as well as in the psychosomatic disequilibrium of their personalities. The minister needs the compassion that Christ had for the demoniac when he starts dealing with these persons. Their communities have often consigned them to the tombs without the advantage of a funeral.

IV. The Level of Teaching

The pastor as a personal counselor finds that some of his most effective teaching is done with individuals in a face-to-face ministry. Jesus most often appeared to his followers as a teacher. The matchless teachings which he left the world were ordinarily the outgrowth of his ministry to individuals who were drawn to him for help. The Christian shepherd functions as an instructor of the conscious minds, the moral intentions, and the undisciplined desires of his people. On the teaching level of his personal ministry, therefore, he needs to know not only the content of Christian teaching and practice, but also the process whereby these become a part of the spiritual tissue of the personalities of his people.

When a person comes to a Christian pastor for guidance in a personal difficulty, he usually expects that pastor to be an interpreter of the mind of Christ, "a teacher come from God." The minister represents this reality to him. Furthermore, the minister is supposed to be an authority on the teachings of the Bible and Christian history, and people come to him with thorny personal problems at the base of questions as to what the Bible teaches about divorce, remarriage, adultery, the unpardonable sin, money matters, profanity, war, and a hundred other things. The minister is expected to know the historical context of Christian experience, and to be able to use this knowledge in a healing way.

The minister, in addition, is supposed to be an authority on the specific teachings and practices of his own Church. Young engaged couples of different religious persuasions come asking him to explain the difference between the teaching and practices of Catholics and Protestants, for instance, and his knowledge and attitude will have a determinative effect upon their decision. The minister also finds himself the interpreter of the social attitudes of his people all the way from such matters as personal amusements that are taboo to world-wide attitudes on race prejudice and war.

On the teaching level of pastoral ministry, the Christian shepherd finds a distinctive characteristic of his work that sets him apart from professional counselors and necessitates a departure from their ideologies. This distinctive, however, brings him closer to the reality of people's problems, i.e., *the pastor represents both the individual's and the group's interests, and he must combine individual and group counseling procedures.* The person-minded minister knows that many of his personal counseling opportunities come as the result of questions he stimulated in group discussions. Conversely, he must confront the " reality principle " of his group connections and those of his counselees in all personal work with individuals.

But people come to their minister not only for guidance on specifically religious questions, but also for information on the common ventures of everyday life. Parents who have not been able to have children want to know adoption procedures. Young people seek premarital instruction. High school graduates want to know about the college facilities available to them. Children of elderly parents want guidance concerning homes for aged people. Relatives of mentally ill persons want guidance concerning psychiatric help and legal procedures involved in institutionalization. Parents invariably want to talk over problems in child guidance with their pastor, seeking information about the simpler as well as the more complex problems in mental hygiene. The request for the recommendation of medical specialists in cases of physical illness is a very common appeal.

In all these instances and countless others, the minister is expected to be a repository of information. As one young minister, after two years of pastoral work, said: " They came to me, but they did not ask me what I *thought*. They said, ' Pastor, do you *know* . . . ? ' " Therefore, the minister should take heed to knowing his Bible, his church, and his community resources. These are his equipment.

The methods of instructional guidance are varied, but in every instance these approaches must be distinguished from long lectures of moralistic exhortations filled with such phrases as: " Don't you know . . . ? " " I think you ought . . ." " Maybe you don't realize it, but . . ." *Instructional guidance is the impartation of facts necessary for the voluntary choice of an individual to work with intelligence.* The use of good books is one of the most tactful methods to be employed here. The pastor should take care to separate heavier volumes that he would use for his own instruction from those briefer, more plainly written books he would use for guiding other people. Likewise, he should not recommend literature before he himself has read it. Every pastor needs a loan shelf of books and pamphlets that he has bought with extra gifts of money that come to him from time to time. He will lose a few this way, but they will be valuable even so. (See Appendix C.)

Supplying missing facts is another method of personal instruction. A pastor may be listening carefully to a mission volunteer who is making his educational plans, but he suddenly realizes that this man is already beyond the age limit for missionaries in the area in which he wants to serve. A member of the official board of the church may want to make a certain change in the financial policy of the church, and the pastor supplies the missing fact that the charter of the church expressly forbids it. This type of counseling is especially valuable to the religious counselor on college campuses and to people who teach in institutions of learning. " The rules " become the grooves on which much of their counseling progresses.

CHAPTER VII

THE LEVELS OF PASTORAL CARE (*Continued*)

The *dialectical method of pastoral care,* styled along the line of the Socratic dialectic, is the most easily used technique of approaching the personal problems of an individual. This method is a common-sense approach to pastoral procedure which is most likely to do good, and the least likely to do harm. It is also a fitting preparatory approach to any "deeper level" counseling that needs to be done. The dialectical method assumes that the help-seeking person is of average intelligence, fairly stable emotionally, and capable of talking freely about his situation with no unusual degree of mental blocking. Further, this method assumes a strong degree of personal rapport between the individual and his pastor, and it is usually appropriate with people to whom the pastor has been related over a period of time as a pastor and teacher. Ordinarily there is a permanent bond of identification between pastor and the person at hand. These are rather sweeping prerequisites for the use of such an approach, and the psychologist or the psychiatrist may ask whether or not there *are* any such people living. But the pastor deals with such people every day of his ministry, whereas these experts rarely see them.

The process of dialectical pastoral care is as follows: First, the pastor simply listens to the parishioner who comes to him in times of decision and lays out a problem before him. He asks an occasional question in order to fill in missing facts. Here, in actuality, *the pastor himself is the student,* much as Socrates was a "student" with the youth of Athens, learning from the person at hand all the facts about the present situation confronting him. He is "leading the person out" (in the Latin sense of the word "education").

Secondly, the pastor gives a *factual summary,* a sort of recapitulation, of what the person has told him. He may initiate this by saying:

" Now let me see whether or not I have all the facts in the matter before me. You have told me . . ." Then upon finishing a concise statement of the facts at hand, he may say: " Do I understand you properly? Have we left anything out? " Quite often the person will say, " Yes, I failed to mention this . . ."

Thirdly, the pastor lines up the *alternative paths of action,* and with the help of the parishioner explores the end results and methods of achieving those results in each one of the alternative paths of action. Usually this may be initiated by asking the question, " Now what are the things you *can* do in the situation? " After carefully enumerating these alternatives, each one can be discussed freely in a give-and-take manner as to obstacles preventing their realization, ways and means of accomplishment, and unique advantages inherent in each choice. Often the condition of things calls for the pastor's adding " another possibility " for the consideration of the individual — a possibility that the person probably has not yet seen. Many times this " other possibility " may be a careful combination of the best advantages of the other alternatives. For instance, a young girl does not know whether to stay in school or to go to work in order that she and her fiancé can marry. Finally she decides to stay in school, lighten her class load, get a part-time job, and marry. Inasmuch as both of them have only one more year, she feels that they can " make it."

The fourth step is to *appeal to the basic desire* of the person. Often the pastor may ask, " If all things were equal, now, which of these alternatives do you really want to follow — deep down inside? " Quite often an amused light comes to the person's eye and he says, " Well, I guess I did not want your advice so much as I wanted sympathy in what I have already decided to do." But on frequent occasions one may be answered: " I guess that is my big problem: I don't know what I want to do. I want to have my cake and eat it too, and I am not able to choose one thing and carry through with it." The more intense this feeling is, the more likely the pastor is to be dealing with a person suffering from some type of psychoneurotic difficulty. At any rate, the " big problem " is out in the open, and the pastor is firmly established in the person's confidence in order that he may go into the deeper difficulties of the individual.

But in the majority of the situations that confront a pastor, this dialectical method of pastoral care produces a heightened degree of emotional maturity, whets the sense of personal responsibility, and leaves the decision-making capacity of the person free and inviolate. By all means it lends itself to one-interview situations most readily, and is adaptable to the pressurized schedules of most pastors.

V. The Level of Pastoral Counseling and Psychotherapy

Not all personal encounters yield themselves to the rational approach suggested in the discussion of the dialectical method of pastoral care. The Christian shepherd confronts many people who are suffering from deep inner conflicts over which they have no control. They stand in need of a minister who has psychological foundation and psychotherapeutic skill in his method as well as the healing power of God at his disposal. Such persons have come to the point where *they do not want to do what they want to do.* Their decision-making powers are deadlocked in a filibuster of *one* of their many selves in the congress of their souls. Unhappy people, they come to the pastor complaining that they cannot control their thoughts and actions. In the thought of Paul, they do not understand their own actions, for they do not the things they want, but do the very things they hate (Rom. 7:15).

Such persons are not "insane" in the sense that people suffer from gross delusions of grandeur and persecution and stand in need of institutionalization and protective care. Accordingly, they are not candidates for a psychiatrist ordinarily, and usually they are not wealthy enough to afford a psychoanalyst who specializes in their troubles. Rather, they are usually people of limited means who are acutely unhappy and blocked out of the abundant life. Nevertheless, they may be conscientious church members and active in the affairs of the community. Their religion, however, seems to be conformed to the pattern of their unhappy way of life, rather than a transforming power that renews their mind.

In order to deal effectively with the basic religious needs that these conflict-weary persons manifest, the pastor must be acquainted with the " heart's native language " of feelings as well as the rational precepts of his theological formulations. As Nathaniel Hawthorne says:

" If he show no intrusive egotism; . . . if he have the power, which must be born with him, to bring his mind into such an affinity with his patients' that this last shall unawares have spoken what he himself imagines himself only to have thought; if such revelations be received without tumult, and acknowledged not so often by an unuttered sympathy as by silence, and inarticulate breath, and here and there a word, to indicate that all is understood; if to these qualifications of a confidant be joined the advantages afforded by his recognized character as a physician; then, at some inevitable moment, will the soul of the sufferer be dissolved and flow in a dark but transparent stream, bringing all its mysteries unto the daylight." [21]

Such a " feeling for the feelings " of people, a careful clinical study of people's troubles, and an equally careful re-examination of the New Testament, reveal a Christian explanation of their difficulties: idolatry in the sphere of values is the basic religious component in the malformations encountered in these particular psychological diseases. The person suffering from a neurotic way of life is a slave " to the elemental spirits of the universe . . . in bondage to beings that by nature are no gods " (Gal. 4:3, 8).

Primarily he is possessed by the demand of one part of himself that the rest of himself bow down in its worship. As Plato said, this type of sin is " the rising up of a part of the soul over the whole." This individual is not a person, but many selves. He condemns himself roundly on every hand, giving the key to his plight when he says: " I could never forgive myself . . ." Thus it is seen clearly that he is an inordinate worshiper of fictitious goals in life, borrowed standards for his life, fantasies of what he thinks himself ideally to be. The viciousness of his idolatry lies in its self-destructiveness, its prating itself as humility, self-denial, self-rejection, and religious devotion. The person's desires to become a person in his own right overshoots the mark and he aspires to become God himself.

[21] *The Scarlet Letter*, p. 128. Pocket Books, Inc.

The only answer to his plight is that the eyes of his inner understanding be opened to the fact of his irresponsibility and of his
childish sense of omnipotence. His inner life must be opened to the
ethically severe love of God, which convinces him that the root of
his sin is in his self-enchantment, that God is consistent and can be
depended upon to work within a person as he makes and carries out
decisions, and that God is a rewarder of them that diligently seek
after him. Such a picture is seen in the life of the man whom Jesus
first asked, before he healed him, " Wilt thou be made whole? " And
the surest thing that a pastor can do for such a conflict-weary person
who comes to him is to put him on his own before God, to give
him all the loving confidence and intelligent affection that he has
time and opportunity to give him.

But a theological orientation to the problems of neurotic people
does not suffice in and of itself. The busy pastor needs a clear concep-
tion of *how* to go about "putting a person on his own before God
and giving him all the intelligent affection that he has time and opportunity to give." Every responsible pastor knows that the neurotic
personalities in his church not only are unhappy themselves, but
cause unhappiness to others all out of proportion to their own number. Careful study of church splits and church failures will reveal
that they are often initiated and perpetuated by chronically malad-
justed people. Therefore, the minister is forced by circumstances to
ask, " What am I going to do for and about the neurotic personalities
in my church? "

In the first place, the minister needs to acquaint himself with the
basic literature in the field of counseling and psychotherapy. Professor Carl Rogers, of the University of Chicago, has written the most
often cited book in the field, *Counseling and Psychotherapy.* In this
book he sets forth what he calls the " client-centered " viewpoint of
counseling. Professor Russell L. Dicks has set forth a practice which
he calls " creative listening " as a method of dealing with fear-ridden,
lonely, guilt-laden people. This description of " creative listening "
is found in his revised edition of *Pastoral Work and Personal Counseling,* and in an article found in *Mental Hygiene,* October, 1948,
in which he says, " If I could use but one method in pastoral work,

I should choose the *listening* method." Also Karen Horney's book, *Our Inner Conflicts,* on the structure of neurotic behavior patterns, has an exceptionally valuable contribution to make to religious thinkers. These three sources, however, will be of invaluable aid to the pastor in formulating his own adapted approach to people with difficulties that are more deeply embedded.

But in actuality, the only effective means of learning the methods described in these books is to enroll in a clinic for the training of pastors. A minister can get this training in his theological curriculum in many schools today, and those that cannot can easily gain access to a training center during a summer. If one is already in a pastoral situation, he can get a leave of absence or commute to the nearest center of training. The various resources for this type of training are described in Appendix A of this book. In such a center of training, a minister becomes a part of the healing team — medical doctors, social workers, psychiatrists, nurses, and ministers are all helpfully related to the same persons in need. Furthermore, he is given close personal supervision in his individual work with people by a trained theological supervisor. Here " the living human documents of flesh and blood " become the textbooks for the minister, and his gospel comes alive to him in the face-to-face ministry to people in need.

Some persons ask, " How far should a pastor go in ' deeper level counseling '? " The answer is threefold: He should go as far as his training has equipped him to accept responsibility for the outcome of his treatment. He can go as far as the uncontrolled environment in which he works will permit him to accept responsibility for the person's life. And, finally, he can go as far as the limitations of his time and social role will permit him to give himself to the needs of the individual.

The therapeutic work of a minister is a dynamic and growing relationship. The pastor does well to think of himself as counseling in the creative processes of spiritual birth and maturation, and to think of the person before him as needing new life and spiritual maturity. This creative process moves naturally through five phases. The phases may take place quickly in one interview, but more often the relationship may extend over several or even a larger number of conferences. This allows time for growth and reflection, during which the person has to deal with his own problems alone.

A. *The Preparatory Phase of Counseling*

The more inexperienced pastor usually asks the question, " How is it that people come to their pastor for counseling help? " The veteran minister asks, " How can I get people who ask for help started off in an effective relationship for the best results in my counseling with them? " Others may ask, " How can I stimulate the need for counseling help in a person who does not yet feel that he either needs help or that I am the person to give it? " All these questions indicate the fact that there is a preparatory phase in most counseling relationships. In this phase the pastor does several things: He first discovers who needs his help, and establishes an initial contact with that person. If the person comes to him in an informal situation, he seeks to construct a more formal one in which time, privacy, and quietness can be achieved. If the person must be sought out by visitation or by cultivation of friendship, the pastor seeks to stimulate the sense of need for help and to " shift the initiative " in the relationship in such a way that the person " stretches forth his own hand " for help.

Discovering persons in need and establishing an initial contact. The pastor is one of the very few persons in modern society who is still expected to visit his people. In some communities even this expectation is losing its strength. But ordinarily, the pastor has a right to visit in the homes of his community, and this is his best means of discovering persons in need and of establishing an initial contact with them. Purposeful and patient home visitation reveals to the observant pastor, especially when he goes in times of crises, many of the quieter and more desperate needs of individuals and families. It establishes rapport that will be necessary to any future counseling. It gives a distinctly personal and nonprofessional touch to the pastor's interest in people. It offers him opportunities to see the individual in the context of the family and to sense the feelings of other members of the family toward that person. Home visitation presents the pastor with a *total pattern* of the way of life of the person which only many hours of individual counseling would ultimately reveal.

Likewise, as has already been indicated in the discussion of preaching and teaching, the pastor's public ministry affords him "after-meeting" conversations with persons who have private matters they wish to discuss. This is the pastoral counselor's "outlet to the sea" of human suffering. Careful, insightful, and humanly tender preaching and teaching are avenues of exchange of feeling between a pastor and the individual who needs personal counseling.

Furthermore, the patient education of the leadership of the church to guide persons in acute need to the pastor rewards him with an abundance of initial contacts with such persons. This is best illustrated by a negative example. A middle-aged woman, who had been married only about six years, became deeply depressed and took her life by self-poisoning. One of her neighbors called the pastor immediately, asking that he make his services available to the husband of the woman in making plans for and conducting the funeral. In the telephone conversation, she said, "I have known for some time that she was thinking of doing such a thing, but I never believed she would!" If the woman had been trained to do so, she could have notified the pastor long *before* the tragedy. As it was, all she knew to do was to call him for the funeral!

Probably the most Christlike method of establishing initial contacts with persons in need is in what may be termed the pastor's "market-place ministry." In the casual, informal contacts of everyday living with people — in the grocery store, in the filling station, at the bank, in the garage, at social gatherings of all kinds — the pastor hears the "uplifted voices" of human need. A young pastor tells this story: He read in his morning paper that a man and woman, both members of his church, were seeking a divorce. That morning he stopped, as his custom was, to get some gasoline at the man's service station. He stood reading his paper inside the man's place of business. The proprietor was posting his books, while the attendant filled the pastor's gas tank. Everything was tensely quiet until the owner of the place looked up and snarled at the pastor: "Well, go on and say it. I know what you are going to say anyhow!" The pastor countered by saying: "I am not sure whether or not you feel that I am your friend. I don't want to say anything unless you feel that my friendship belongs to you."

The man was taken aback by this approach. Then he broke into a warm, anguished outpouring of his difficulties with his wife that had culminated in divorce proceedings. The pastor did not try to deal with it at that moment, but said: "I will take good care of your confidence in me. Do you think you and I could get together tonight, after your station closes, and talk this over?" An appointment was made, and the more formal kind of counseling relationship had been established.

This latter step suggests one of the important essentials of the preparatory phase of counseling work: *the pastor should be very effective in the use of an appointment system.* Unless it is otherwise unavoidable, he should not attempt to deal with intimately personal problems of individuals in public places where other people can surmise and draw their own conclusions. He should make appointments, either to visit the person at his own home or in the pastor's study. Such a simplified procedure will do much toward making his time more valuable to others and to himself. This is much wiser than setting arbitrary office hours for people to come to see the pastor if they need help on their personal problems. It is more personal, less of an affront to the autonomy of the people of the community, and therefore less likely to create unnecessary hostility. But more important than this, such a plan does much toward " structuring " the relationship of the pastor to the individual in such a way that he can counsel with him without too many personal obstructions arising.

The most difficult problem that a pastor faces in the preparatory phases of counseling is that of switching the initiative from the pastor to the person whom he is seeking to help. This is more easily illustrated than it is defined. For instance, a young woman called her pastor, asking for an appointment *for her husband* to come and talk with him about some marital problems in which they were involved. The pastor, in the preparatory phases of the counseling relationship, said: "I will be glad to talk with *him* as to a time that is convenient for both of us. Have him call me about it." The purpose of the pastor was to shift the initiative away from the wife and to the husband in the search for help.

Sometimes, a pastor will recognize an acute need in a person in his community, but at the same time the person is hostile and resistant to any help that comes his way. The pastor is confronted with the responsibility of lessening the hostility and uncovering a desire for his guidance. This is one of the most difficult relationships a pastor confronts. For example, a pastor learned that one of the members of his church had made a vow that he would never return to church after seeing his father, the senior elder of the church, with " another woman sitting in my dead mother's place," as the man himself stated.

The pastor visited the home of the man regularly, inasmuch as the man was physically ill a good portion of his time. No mention was ever made of the fact that he did not come to church, the fact that the pastor knew of the conflict between him and his father, and the fact of his father's remarriage. The pastor " waited him out " until the man himself felt secure enough in his affections to tell him about it without being asked. At this point, the man sought the pastor's guidance and became permanently receptive of his counseling help.

Another situation in pastoral care and personal counseling that calls for a switch of initiative is that of moral offenses of a major proportion among persons in the congregation. This usually comes to the pastor's attention in rumors from different persons within the community. Whispers of embezzlement, shady business dealings, sexual promiscuity, sexual perversions, and any of the catalogues that each community compiles come to the ears of the minister as he moves about. Next, the person's place of authority and leadership in the church is questioned, and a rift in the unity of the congregation is in the making. In smaller congregations, the whole unsavory situation can come to a head in a clash of personalities in the open meetings of the church. The pastor's own leadership may become so involved that he may seek to resign.

Such a situation may best be handled in the rumor stage by a pastor who has a firm hand in dealing with people. The pastor may do as one reports in a case record:

Pastor: Wilhelm, I called and asked you to come by to see me for a reason. Before I tell you what I have on my mind, I want to say that my confidence in you as a person runs pretty deep and my affection for you is true and sure. Otherwise, I would not have been concerned about you. Then, too, I want to assure you that no one else knows that you are here, and that all you say to me is in the strictest of confidence.

You may justly tell me, when I say what I have on my mind, that I am sticking my nose into your business and have no right to do so. You will be right except in the fact that I would want you to do for me what I am trying to do for you, because I feel that you are my friend.

Now to come to the point, before you lose your patience in curiosity, let me say that I am not concerned about the truth or error of the reports that have come to me. They could be false and still do you harm. If they are false, I think you are entitled to know that these things are being said. If they are true, I think you are entitled to a sympathetic friend with whom you can talk in confidence about your side of the story. There are, as you well know, two sides to all such things.

The word has come to me that you have been engaging in sexual perversions with some of the young boys and girls in our church. The exact situations are these: _____; _____; _____; _____. I will not tell you who told me all this, because I do not want to do all of you harm. But you can imagine for yourself, and if this is not true, you can be secure in knowing that they do not know that I am talking to you either.

What do you think about all this?

Wilhelm: Well, for a good while I have wanted to talk with you about this, but I never knew quite how to go about it. I have been doing some of those things. Not all of them, though. I came here a stranger and thought I had found a really Christian crowd that didn't do those things. I got into it, though, and found that they were not so different from myself. . . .

The conclusion of the whole history is too lengthy to report in full, but this part of the record indicates that rapport was established and that the preparatory phases of such counseling can move from an authoritarian to a permissive realtionship between the counselor and the counselee. The pastor may have many difficulties in dealing with such a problem in the next phases that are to be discussed, but at least he has " structured " his relationship in such a way that the initiative is with the counselee more than it is with the pastor.

B. *The Phase of Relaxation and Rapport*

Most persons who are suffering from emotional handicaps are tense, suspicious, and self-conscious. In the earliest phases of the pastor's relationship to such persons, he faces the necessity of putting them at ease and disarming them of their personal mistrust of him. Likewise, he necessarily must establish some meeting point of feeling with the person and define clearly his own relationship to the person. The success or failure of a counseling situation is often determined within the first half hour of the discussion; the "relationship of a trusted motive" must be established, and the suspicions of the person relieved before progress can be made.

The pastor in this phase of any relationship, therefore, will be sensitive to three factors in the experience of the person with whom he is conferring:

1. *The degree of nervous tension.* Breathlessness may indicate either fear of the interview situation or haste in making the appointment in time. Drawn features may indicate sleeplessness and loss of appetite. Clenched fists, sweaty palms, and twisted handkerchiefs may point toward a burden of unrelieved anxiety. Rigid perching on the edge of a chair, furtive movements of the body — all these and a hundred other signs are the tattered edges of a tense spirit showing themselves. A pastor must be alert and sensitive to the degree of tension in his people at all times. By the composure within himself, the unhurriedness of his manner, and the steady certainty of his tone of voice, he can communicate confidence and a quietened peacefulness to the person. Often the pastor will purposely avoid talking about significant and painful matters until the person feels more at ease and under less tension. The person must be relatively free from mental blocking that arises from emotional tension before he can with profit discuss his difficulties. This process of relaxation, by whatever legitimate means the pastor most aptly can use, is the first prerequisite of good therapeutic work. The use of small talk, superficial conversation about places and relations, the use of a brief prayer for peace and clarity of vision, and the direct use of suggestions such as: " Sit in this chair. I think you will be able to relax more." " Why not pause a little while

and catch your breath? You have been running." " Lean back in your chair and take it easy." All these point toward an easing of tension.

2. *The degree of personal antagonism*. The occasion that brings many people with deep-seated emotional disturbances to a minister quite often is one of anger and resentment. As has already been mentioned (see Chapter V), such persons come to the pastor under pressure from someone else and resent both that other person and the pastor for putting him into such a position. But occasionally the point that stimulated the person's anger may be something that the pastor himself has done, which he did not like.

Ordinarily the resentment is not a conscious one, but rather lies deeper than the person himself can sense. This is what Freud so aptly called " resistance." Deep wells of antagonism prevent the person from having a relaxed relationship to the pastor. The most common fear is that the minister will condemn the person if he makes himself known as he really is, or that the minister will betray what he knows about him. But even more subtle are those antagonisms which cause persons unconsciously to misinterpret the words of the minister, to ascribe to him meanings that he did not reflect to them, and even to deny the truth of their own words that might be repeated back to them verbatim.

The minister also has the task of disarming his parishioner of any antagonism he may have had toward former ministers and may be unconsciously carrying over into the person's feelings toward him. The resentments that the person holds toward other people in the church also serve as inhibiting obstructions to a friendly relationship.

By careful definition of his own relationship and gentle and anticipatory reassurances of confidence, the minister can tactfully disarm the person of resistance. Sometimes this may take a whole interview; with others a " meeting point of feeling " is never established. But no smoothness of ministry can be achieved until the thermostats of the person's heart have been opened by the warmth of friendship, and sustained by the strength of confidence.

3. *Degree of personal responsibility*. One hazard in the establishment of rapport is that the person will shirk his own personal re-

sponsibility for his difficulties and shift to a complete dependence upon the pastor for their solution. Whereas some people refuse to trust a minister at all, a great many take the relationship of mutual trust as a parasitic opportunity " to pass the buck " of their troubles over to the pastor. When he fails to measure up to their expectations, he begins to get resistance from them. This is the genius of the client-centered principle of counseling: it leaves the responsibility for the solution of the problem with the person who brings it, and provides a permissive and warmly personal atmosphere in which he can objectively work through to a satisfactory solution. Religiously stated, it is the careful observance of the principle of the autonomy of the individual personality before God, and a confident trust in the lawful working of the Holy Spirit " both to will and to work for his good pleasure " in the life of the person.

From the point of view of the pastor, he must take preventive measures in order that he may not become so encumbered with the difficulties of one person that he cannot minister to the many other people who come to him. It aids him in his own personal relaxation to get over *the compulsive necessity to do something about every problem that is brought to him,* and to accept the realism of Paul's maxim, " Each man will have to bear his own load " (Gal. 6:5). The sense in which he is fulfilling the law of Christ by bearing the other person's load with him lies in his provision of a friendly presence of togetherness with the person. Thus he is neither alone nor wrapped up in himself; he is sharing the reality of the Christian community.

These three problems: the degree of tension, the degree of personal antagonism, and the degree of personal responsibility, are the issues at stake in establishing rapport with the person who comes to the pastor with a more profound personality problem. At all stages of counseling, the degree of rapport may be strengthened or weakened in such a way as to help or hinder any further progress. No smoothness of ministry can be achieved at all, however, until the person has made room in his heart for the pastor through the warmth of friendship and the power of confidence.

C. *The Phase of Listening and Exploration*

Overlapping the phase of relaxation and the building of rapport is the period of "talking it out" in "an experience of emotional release, when the person uses the acceptance and permissiveness of the situation to pour out, or painfully to bring out, all the attitudes which surround his life problems. As he discovers that this is a situation in which it is safe to express real feelings, deeper and deeper attitudes are revealed, even those which have been previously repressed and which he has never dared admit even to himself." [22] The person socializes, often for the first time in his life, the thoughts and feelings that have hovered in the hinterlands of his consciousness, creating anxieties which he could not explain but only feel and respond to with blind compulsion.

1. *The ministry of listening.* The pastor at this phase of the therapeutic situation depends almost entirely upon the ministry of listening. Much needs to be said at this point on the use of this powerful tool of pastoral work.

The easiest way to help people is to understand them. As Lin Yutang has said, "To understand is to forgive." The easiest way to understand them is to listen to them, "to hear them out." Listening creatively is an art in itself, because it calls into action those other forms of expression which are dramatically more powerful than the use of words: eye expression, bodily responses of muscle and movement to meaning, and the effect of total silence. As Reik has said, "It is important that we recognize what speech conceals and what silence reveals." [23] Listening essentially means three things:

(*a*) It means *actually to hear what the person says,* to hear with an "evenly hovering attention." Pastors are most susceptible to letting their attention wander from the person to whom they are listening to any one of the thousand other things that they have to think about. Preoccupation with other things is like damp rot in the counseling ministry of a pastor. The shuffling of papers on the desk,

---

[22] Carl R. Rogers, *A Counseling Viewpoint,* pp. 13, 14. Federal Council of Churches.

[23] Theodor Reik, *Listening with the Third Ear,* p. 126.

the searching out of a letter from the pocket, the furtive glance at the watch — all these are subtle ways of telling a person that no attention is being given to what he says. Likewise, the pastor quite often misses the mark in his understanding of his people, because he does not pay close attention to seemingly insignificant details concerning their attitudes and feelings.

But it would be a mistake to assume, as Reik says again, that " all observation is purely conscious. Not until we have learned to appreciate the significance of unconscious observation, reacting to the faintest impressions with the sensitiveness of a sheet of tin foil, shall we recognize the difficulty of transforming imponderabilia into ponderabilia." [24] In this sense, listening is a sort of " free-floating attention," which " makes note of everything equally."

(b) *Listening means letting the person do the talking*. The pastor suffers the temptation to make comments and observations to the person with whom he is counseling, giving them freely his own understanding of the difficulties *as soon as he himself has seen them.* A careful restraint and an attentive listening instead often reveal that the person has already thought of these things himself. It is almost a miracle to hear a person say that which it seemed impossible for him even to see, much less to articulate.

In the sense of *letting* a person do the talking, listening is a passive process. Here the passive listening of the pastor lays hold of the " active power of silence," which " makes small talk transparent, and has a force that pulls the person forward, driving him into deeper layers of his experience than he had intended." Also, it calls upon the initiative of the person to deal with his own dilemmas rather than to rest supinely upon the initiative of the pastor.

Of course, the use of silence, in the sense of letting the person do the talking himself, depends upon the degree of rapport that the pastor has with the person at hand. Reik has pointed out that there are different kinds of silence:

" It is tempting to use the insight into the psychology of silence as a ladder that can be put aside as soon as we have descended to the depths. There are, of course, different kinds of silence; yes, there are even degrees

[24] *Ibid.*, p. 142.

of silence. We speak of a cold, oppressive, defiant, disapproving or con-
demning, as well as of a calming, approving, humble, excusing, silence.
The concept seems to unite opposite meanings, presenting itself with
plus and minus signs. Compare, for instance, 'silence gives consent'
with the rejecting silence of a lady to a man who is forward or objec-
tionable.

" Silence can be conceived of as an expression of quiet sympathy or intense hate. To be silent with a person may mean that we feel quite in
agreement with him or that every possibility of agreement is excluded.
Talkativeness as well as reticence appears as a character trait of the women
whom men love. Lear disavows Cordelia, who loves and is silent, but
Coriolanus returning to his wife tenderly calls her, ' My gracious silence.'
The contrast between speaking and being silent was originally not as
sharp as we might think. We are reminded of the characteristic of an-
cient languages (for instance, of the Egyptian) of forming words with
antithetical meanings so that only a small change later indicated a differ-
entiation of the opposites (compare, for instance, Latin *clamare* = to
shout, *clam* = secretly; German *Stimme* = voice, *stumm* = mute). We
have to assume that silence is primal and that speaking emerged from
silence as life from the inorganic, from death. If we live here on ' borrowed time,' all our speaking is but a fleeting interruption of the eternal
silence. We have to believe with the Gospel of John that in the beginning
was the word, but before that was the great silence. Carlyle, in *On
Heroes and Hero-Worship,* says that speech is of time; silence is of
eternity." [25]

The silence of a physician of the soul " slowly changes its significance to the person with whom he is working." This writer was
interviewing a thirty-year-old man who had always been completely
dependent upon his pastors, college professors, and parents for the
motivation of his behavior. The interviews consisted of many long
and painful silences in between jerky, halting outbursts of insight
into this infantile dependence upon others. On the fourth interview,
the man said, " I have decided that I have been coming to talk with
you just to get on the good side of you, just as I did with my pastor
and my professors in college."

Then the writer said, " You feel that you have been pretty eager
to have my approval? " Then a long, stringent silence ensued, at
the beginning of which the writer felt a sense of impatience at the

[25] *Ibid.,* p. 124.

fact that the man would not talk any further. Then he remembered that silence could uncover what speech would hide, remained silent, and felt the impulse to pray silently in the man's behalf. During the meditative silence, the man arose from his seat and walked out of the room.

Two weeks later, the man sought another conference and told the writer this: "During that exceedingly talkative [laughing at his own humor] interview we had the last time we were together, I made up my mind that, in order to clear my own thinking, I would just have to break my dependence on you. I felt that the only way to do this was to come in and engage you in conversation and get up and walk out and leave you. But when I came, you just sat silent. *At first I felt that your silence was an unfriendly silence, but suddenly it changed and I felt it was a friendly silence. I had the feeling that if I did leave your office, you would understand."*

Therefore, the use of a passive listening is predicated upon the "friendliness of the silence" of the pastor. This can best be approximated by facial assurances of understanding, and by "creating the illusion of talking" with such interjections as, "Uh-huh," "Yes," "I see," "Did he?" Or it can be accomplished by repeating the trailing ends of sentences such as, "You say you went from home to work that morning." This is a continual flow of encouragement from the pastor to the person with whom he is counseling which stimulates the person's confidence to talk and makes it easier. If, however, the pastor is preoccupied with trying to formulate what he himself is going to say as soon as he finds an opening, he may find the opening sooner than he thinks.

(*c*) *Listening, in the third place, means that the pastor actually gets the person to talk.* In this sense, listening is an active experience on the part of the pastor. Here he takes some positive initiative. It is at this point that the pastoral counselor parts company with the "nondirective" approach of Carl Rogers. In the first instance, the pastor can take the initiative in the listening by "following the lead" of the person, and picking up the specific "trailing end" of the sentence that is spoken with the most feeling and strength of tone. This amounts to asking the person to talk a little bit more about that particular subject, without putting it into those words at all.

Again, active listening calls into action the right of a pastor to ask questions. Russell Dicks calls this " directive listening " and says that what the " scalpel is to the surgeon the question is to the pastoral counselor, and it is quite as dangerous. . . . The good pastor is one who knows what to ask and what not to ask, plus a feeling for time-liness." [26] The important thing for a pastor to remember is that he should not run ahead of the sense of rapport that he has with the person, and that he should not ask a question that the person has not given him the spiritual privilege to ask. Then, for the sake of time and because of the informal nature of most pastoral counseling, the pastor can with safety for all concerned encourage the person to talk by asking well-placed questions. Here he may fill out a gap of information, he may reflect a feeling, or he may even suggest an association by the way he asks a question.

These are the three significant meanings of the listening ministry, which should be borne in mind as the pastor enters upon the phase of counseling that has been called " listening and exploration." How-ever, certain precautions as to the use of a passive or active listening approach need to be made. Such a method may cause the pastor to spend time that should be used more valuably by a more skilled per-son who could give more concentrated attention to the person. An example of this would be those persons who are so acutely depressed that they become more agitated and depressed as they talk more. An attempt on the part of the minister to explore their difficulties through a listening approach might even precipitate a suicide. This illustration points to the fact that a total dependence upon listening as a pastoral procedure, to the exclusion of intelligent reassurance and instruction is dangerous.

2. *The achievement of insight.* The frank objective of the pastor in this second phase of the ministry of healing is that the person with whom he is dealing will achieve insight into and develop per-sonal control over his difficulties. This is done by indirection rather than frontal assaults on the besetting difficulties of the individual.

[26] *Mental Hygiene,* October, 1948, p. 580.

It comes to pass through the process of listening and exploration after this manner:

(a) There is a *return of the repressed memories and present feelings of the person*. It is a mistake to think of these memories as being *past* experiences. They live actively in the present existence of the individual, and he unconsciously considers them as present realities rather than things that are in the past. As one patient, in a hospital, upon having dreamed of her childhood, said, "All those people who are supposed to be dead are now alive in my mind." These are buried memories, yes, but they were buried alive, and, like Hamlet's father's uneasy spirit, find their way back into the daily affairs of the person's life. The ministry of attentive, careful, and considerate listening provides the atmosphere in which these memories and present feelings may return for the conscious consideration of the person himself and for later assimilation into his reasonable way of life. The Gestalt psychologists, with uncanny insight, have called these experiences and feelings "an unassimilated mass."

(b) There is an *expression of ambivalent feelings on the part of the person*. This means simply that the person has opposing feelings about the same object of concern: he may say in one context that he almost worships his father, and in another connection say that he has discovered recently that his father is dismally wrong about many things. In the presence of the contradictions, the pastor may be prone to say, "But I thought you said you almost worshiped him!" This would give the person a trapped feeling that might break rapport, and justly so. Rogers wisely suggests that *simply to reflect these feelings back to the person in a mirror-fashion brings best results*. Whereas they see through a glass darkly, and know only in part, this is a way of moving them toward a completion of their insight. As Carl Rogers says:

"Where the client is conflicted in his feelings, where both love and hostility, attraction and repulsion, or both sides of a difficult choice, are being expressed, it is particularly important to recognize this clearly as an ambivalent attitude. Some of the sorts of recognition which may be given are exemplified in such statements as, 'You feel you should go into commerce, but music is the thing you really like'; 'In spite of your bitterness toward your father, you do like him'; 'You want to come for help, yet still at times you feel that it is too difficult for you.'" [27]

This acceptance, clarification, and balancing of contradictory needs in the person's life is one of the vital phases of the achievement of insight. Especially is this true in people's feelings toward God. The tension between the need for aggression and the need for passivity, the need for independence and the need for dependence, the need for individuality and the need for social approval, the need for rebellion and the need for authority constantly calls for a sense of spiritual balance. The achievement of this balance in the lives of his people is a frankly accepted objective of a good pastor.

(c) The *need for self-rejection and the need for self-acceptance* constantly tend to stalemate each other. These opposing needs usually appear in the context of the question that arises as to whether the person at hand should express himself or deny himself in his search for personal satisfaction. He may have in mind his aggressive impulses and say that he feels very guilty over losing his temper, but that he cannot accept himself as a " Mr. Milquetoast "! Or he may realize that he has freedom in Christ to enjoy his sexual life, but that he does not know what to do with his freedom. Of course, all such instances again are illustrations of ambivalent feelings toward the self. They reflect a fear of one's own emotions and a confusion as to one's purposes in life.

Naturally, the problems of self-acceptance are basically of a religious nature.[28] They suggest that the achievement of insight in the process of personal counseling may be superficial or profound, destructive or creative, temporary or permanent, depending upon the level of truly religious feeling it reaches. *The Christian pastor frankly accepts the fact that ethical values make a difference in the mental health of a person.* Discriminating judgment of such values reveals about four qualitatively different levels of insight:

(a) *The ascetic level of insight.* Here the individual refuses to accept the fact that he even has negative feelings of aggression, pas-

[27] *Counseling and Psychotherapy,* pp. 147, 148.
[28] Robert H. Bonthius, *Christian Paths to Self-acceptance.* King's Crown Press, 1948.

sionate feelings of a sexual nature, power drives of domination, and acquisitive desires for possession. He lives on the basis of complete repression and inner blindness to his humanity. In a word, he feels not only that he is without sin, but that he is not tempted.

(b) *The fatalistic level of intellectual insight.* On this level the individual is " sicklied o'er with the pale cast of thought," accepts intellectually that he has certain problems, but finds more satisfaction in analyzing himself than in attempting any changes in his way of life. Quite often he will use the opportunity for an interview as a mirror before which he can preen his symptoms. It is as though he had a filmlike image of himself before him, and his descriptions of his difficulties were means of satisfaction rather than an unhappiness to him. Again, such a person may subtly defy the counselor to solve his problems and when the house is swept clean, he may return a few days later with " seven other " problems to take the place of the first one.

Or the person may take a fatalistic attitude of a stoic and become one whose " head is bloody, but unbowed," engage in heroics of his determination, and resign himself to his fate.

(c) *The perverted level of Machiavellian insight.* On this level the person sees his antisocial and asocial tendencies and rejoices in the new freedom of his insight. He takes his knowledge as an occasion to the flesh and sets about to make up for time he lost as an ascetic. He takes a delinquent turn, and the people around him pay the price for his new-found understanding of himself. His insight is that of the perverted wisdom of the serpent. He takes advantage of society to get his own wishes, although he may use the appearance of socially acceptable standards to get his own way.

(d) *The level of the Christian stewardship of insight.* On this profoundest level of insight, the person comes to the conclusion that he is willing to give up immediate pleasures for more lasting and eternal satisfactions, that he will use his impulses as " instruments of righteousness " unto life rather than instruments of sin unto death. He interprets his own good in terms of the social feeling he has for other people, and uses his new-found freedom as a means to liberate and understand those about him. He alleviates their suffering even as his has been alleviated for him. This sounds the depths of Christian experience, and lays hold of the need of the individual for community with other people who share in the fellowship of shared values, also. Here the individual has achieved insight not only into the nature of his own imperfections and lack of omnipotence, but he also has entered into an acceptance of the imperfections and fallibilities of those about him. He has come to accept temporal reality in its proper relation to the Eternal.

The achievement of such insight moves from " deep . . . unto deep " in the reality of the counseling situation. The pastor needs to be very careful not to accept the first statement of a problem as the real one, because this is very rarely true. For instance, a young university student came on the first interview saying that he had begun to doubt " that God exists." Then on the third interview, without any interruption at all, he said, " I have no doubt that God exists and that he is good, but I am beginning to see that my real trouble is that I am afraid my father and mother will not approve my marrying until I finish school." On the fourth interview, he said, " I guess my main problem is that my mother has never wanted me to marry." On a later interview he said, " I am going ahead with my plans to be married this summer, and I think I can help mother to take it."

The problem in this instance changed its form in the student's mind as the level of his insight deepened. Like Job, he did not begin to lay hold of the resources of strength until he sought help for those who were at one and the same time the closest to him and his greatest vexation.

D. *The Phase of Reconstruction and Guidance*

The pastor is concerned, not only with helping persons with their inner conflicts, but also with their reconstruction of purposes, and their need for guidance in a new way of life. The task of reorganization of personality is essentially a therapeutic one, whereas the task of helping that person back into action is one of education and guidance. Therefore, the pastor, in this third phase of his counseling ministry, is on hand when the person begins to formulate a plan of action in a new way of living. Consequently, his approach may change considerably in order that he may meet the new needs of the person.

Usually the pastor succeeds most often if he appeals to the sense of adventure and experimentation of the person with whom he is dealing at the time. Several issues present themselves at this stage of the relationship:

1. He may want to give a *brief interpretation* of the basic causes of the trouble, or make a series of concrete suggestions. It is best that these be terse, to the point, in simple language, and easily understood. *Usually, as in all phases of personal counseling, it is better to use the same words that the person himself uses and to lay hold of any figures of speech or ways of expression that he himself has presented.* The writer is reminded of a member of one of his rural churches who once asked him " what to do when the plow hits a stump and a fellow swears before he can stop to save his life." Being in the midst of the preparation of a sermon on temptation, the writer went into a long, detailed, catacomblike explanation of how to stop swearing. The man listened with interest and attention, and when the pastor had finished he said, " Yes, but, pastor, by the time I remember all that, I've done gone and cussed! "

Several tested ways of interpretation are valuable: A pastor may interpret by the kind of questions he asks, the order in which he asks them, and the tone of voice in which he speaks. The interview which Jesus held with the woman at the well of Samaria is a case in point here. He interpreted her problem by asking her to go get her husband. Again, a pastor may interpret by giving a short summary of the relationship and the different turns the conversation has taken. Another method which Jesus used constantly was that of an appeal to the experience of other people, the use of a parable, or the use of a proverb. Sometimes the parables the persons themselves use are invaluable. One person said that his life was like the wagon full of barrels which they used to haul water from the river to the church baptistry: by the time it got to the church, all the water that had been in the back barrel was in the front and vice versa. He averred that his family discord had so affected his work, and vice

versa, that he could not tell which was which! This is a valuable
" homemade parable " for use in interpretation.

But the best way that a pastor can interpret the life situation of a
person to him is to discuss frankly and objectively the personal responses of affection and antipathy that the person expresses toward
him as a counselor. This is called " using the transference." An illustration of it is the young woman who, for several years, had moved
from one denomination to another as she became attached to a different pastor. In bringing her difficulty to the pastor in mind at
this particular time, she finally came to the conclusion that she would
unite with his church. He registered no surprise nor undue elation.
On the next interview, the pastor was able to interpret tactfully what
her changing denominations had meant to her and to disentangle
her church affiliation from too much dependence upon ministers.

2. The pastor may be asked by the person to whom he is ministering to confer with him on a specific plan of action with reference to
marriage, parental responsibilities, educational plans, or vocational
readjustments. Here he may resort to the *dialectical method of counseling* which has been suggested earlier in this chapter. At the
same time, he may take on the functions of an evangelist, in the
strict use of that word also, to relate the person to the church, to
fellowship groups, and to other sources of spiritual undergirding.
Likewise, he may feel that some member of his church or community, such as a doctor, a lawyer, a businessman and employer, or
maybe one of the dependable women of the church could be of use
to this person. Therefore, he may refer him to one or more of these
friends for specialized help.

At this stage of the counseling process, the pastor also may deem
it advisable to refer the person to certain literature that will be specifically applicable to his reconstruction of his outlook on life. He
may find that the person knows next to nothing about the Bible and
that he has the opportunity to cause the New and Old Testaments
to come alive to the person in the light of his own life situation. By
and large, the persons who come to a pastor are religious illiterates
and stand in need of this sort of help. The pastor should be very
careful not to hand the whole Bible to people and make some gener-

alized and vague remark as to its healing power. He should carefully (ahead of time if possible) select the sections that give the clearest guidance to the person in terms of his educational background.

Whatever interpretation, instruction, or referral is given to the person should be a plain path of action. The person will need reassurance, spiritual support, and vital encouragement. The therapeutic power of the pastor's own confidence in the person cannot be overestimated. The pastor, however, needs to use down-to-earth common sense in suggesting goals as he evolves plans along with the person. These goals need to be in keeping with the abilities of the person to achieve them. All these procedures are appropriate only after the pastor and the parishioner together have a relaxed sense of certainty that they have arrived at the real issues of the person's life situation. If the pastor has any doubt at all that the person has not come to the core of the problem with him, or if he is confused in his own mind as to what the situation actually is, he should begin to " angle " for another interview. Reflection, maturation, and the opportunity for more conversation are the only things that can clarify the matter.

E. *The Phase of Follow-up and Experimentation*

Much effective counseling has gone to waste because of a failure to follow up the progress of the persons with whom pastors have dealt. This is notoriously true of the counseling done by pastors in evangelistic meetings. In this final phase of personal counseling, several issues are at stake:

1. The breaking of the continuity of regular interviews creates an emotional crisis in the life of the person in and of itself. The chances are that the person has become too dependent upon the counselor, and the interviews have become something of a sedative to soothe his anxieties. He may interpret the breaking of a series of formal interviews as a personal rejection. At this point, the pastor is made to feel more keenly the powerful charges of affection that have been transferred to him by the person. One person said to his pastor, " What will I do when you are too far away for me to find you? "

The pastor interpreted his relationship in this manner: "You seem to wish that I were capable of being everywhere, and probably are assuming that I am all-powerful, also, as far as you are concerned. This is your attempt to deify me, but only God can be God in your life. It is he who is all-present and all-powerful, and you can talk with him any time. We call this prayer, and I should like for you to develop that practice in your life." The Christian pastor, in his ministry of "follow-up" can do nothing more effective than to tutor the people with whom he counsels in the art of prayer. This can be done on a group as well as an individual basis.

Another difficulty of an overdependent relationship between a pastor and a parishioner at the point of follow-up is that the person will continue to bring each minor decision to him for his opinion or for an opportunity to sustain the former continuity. This is especially true of pastors or student counselors in a college setting. Adolescents draw a great deal of personal strength from being near a person with whom they can identify and like whom they would seek to become. They have an abundance of "free-floating" anxiety that they allay in this way when they are away from home and those people who have naturally filled voids in their lives.

2. The failure to provide room for false starts and mistakes and relapses to old patterns of behavior by holding over the person's head a perfectionistic, "sure-cure" goal to be achieved may cause the person to avoid the pastor in the event such things should happen. He feels that, if he makes one slip, he would not dare face the pastor who had such high hopes for him. He may come back later and say that he has "let the pastor down." In a real sense he has let his pastor displace God on this score also.

Another way of falling into the same error is to dominate the person's decision in such a way that the only way he can become a person in his own right is to rebel completely against the whole relationship with the pastor. In the context of a pastoral community, such rebellions can take vicious turns and do more damage than can be undone in a long while.

3. The gossip hazard also conditions the form that a "follow-up" ministry may take. The parishioner may become very uneasy as he

gets more removed from the face-to-face relationship to the minister. Then he will become apprehensive lest the confidences he imparted to his pastor be given away to others. Out of sheer discomfort, he may move his church membership to another church. Or, in the pressure of a momentary crisis, he may seek out irresponsible persons in the community and give an emotionally distorted version of some snatch of his conversation with the pastor. Jesus, in his pastoral ministry, was continually plagued by the results of such gossip. Little wonder that he charged people to go and tell no man of their interview!

4. But more positively, the pastor may follow up his private conferences with people by visits in the home. He has this privilege and will often be invited into the homes of his new-found friends. He may be invited to perform the wedding ceremony of the young man or woman whom he counseled prior to the marriage. These same persons will occasionally invite him to conduct a dedication service in their new home or when a baby is born to them. A young minister may ask him to preach his "ordination sermon," or a young businessman may want him to speak at his civic club. Besides all these outside contacts, the majority of the persons with whom a pastor counsels will be members of his church and he will see them in services, have them in discussion groups, and preach to them Sunday after Sunday. These contacts can enrich or impoverish the counseling ministry of the pastor, depending upon his appreciation of the dynamics of group life and his sensitivity to his people's feelings toward each other.

Quite often the minister will counsel with people whom he will not see again because they are not so closely knit with his own community. They may be people from another city who have been sent to him by some person whom he has helped before and who has moved away. They may be the relatives of a member of his church who have been hospitalized in the city where the pastor ministers. Or, they may come to him from having read something he wrote, having heard him over the radio, or having seen him in a religious assembly meeting. As one "person-minded" minister wrote: "I sometimes wonder how it is the word gets around about one, if he is competent to help others when they need him. But I am learning daily how much it does get around. I count it a privilege to counsel with them, but I am constantly amazed at my total inadequacy — but by leaning hard on the counsel of the Holy Spirit, the friend and I work out in our thinking helpful avenues through many and varied problems."

This seems to define the feeling of a minister who is concerned with the inner peace of his people: He feels competent and full of confidence in his ministry; yet he senses his inadequacy as he confronts the magnitude of human suffering; when he discovers his own perennial source of dependence in the Holy Spirit and a sense of community with the person in need, helpful avenues are found.

A minister can never become overconfident of his own skill in the use of any technique of pastoral care. If he does, he soon begins to depreciate and think irreverently of the personalities of those with whom he deals. He begins to " play on their souls," which causes them to turn on him to rend him. Shakespeare describes such careless irreverence in Hamlet's dialogue with Rosencrantz and Guildenstern, who had been sent to lure his secret from him. He begged Guildenstern tauntingly to play upon a flute which he offered him. But Guildenstern said: " I have not the skill. . . . These cannot I command to any utterance of harmony." Then, with much vehemence, Hamlet replied:

" Why, look you now, how unworthy a thing you make of me! You would play upon me, you would seem to know my stops, you would pluck out the heart of my mystery, you would sound me from my lowest note to the top of my compass; and there is much music, excellent voice, in this little organ, yet cannot you make it speak. 'Sblood, do you think that I am easier to be play'd on than a pipe? Call me what instrument you will, though you can fret me, you cannot play upon me." [29]

[29] *Hamlet,* Act III, Scene 2.

CHAPTER VIII

THE PASTOR AS A MEMBER OF A "COMMUNITY TEAM"

The Christian pastor cannot work alone. He does not minister to his flock without soon finding that he is not the only person in the community who is concerned with the welfare of his parishioners. Nor is he alone in the depth of his devotion to people, in the clarity of his sense of mission in the world, and in the favor of those to whom he ministers. Within the context of the Christian community in a large city may be found *many* ministers who have " gifts that differ accordingly" from those of the pastor of the congregation, such as employers, landowners, teachers, lawyers, medical doctors, psychiatrists, social workers, clinical psychologists, and — most important of all — parents. In the rural community, the consolidated school staff, the athletic coach, the county agent, the home demonstration agent, the general medical practitioners, and parents give in a less complex manner these same ministries.

Often the fascinating vocations of these people pull them away from rather than bind them closer to the church. The mechanistic education of many highly trained specialists sometimes has driven a wedge between their present way of life and the original sense of mission with which they started, and which often was stimulated by the church. Many times the careless neglect and unfriendly harshness from the pastors of these valuable persons have further alienated them from a vital Christian activity. But most of all, they have not been made to feel that their skill and resources are indispensable necessities to the total witness of the church to the community. They have thought of the church as the one-man activity of the pastor rather than as the co-operative teamwork of all the members in a ministry to the total personality of individuals according as each man has need.

Therefore, the Christian pastor's task, upon having come to a new community, is to make friends first with his fellow shepherds, i.e., the other pastors of the community regardless of denomination; secondly, with the physicians, surgeons, and psychiatrists in the community; thirdly, with the social workers, heads of institutions, and public-school teachers; fourthly, with the parent-teacher organizations and child-care agencies; and, of course, the parent of any child should be considered by the pastor as his greatest ally in the spread of the gospel. These are all members of a "community team" of healing helpfulness to people. As a general rule, they, like the minister, are passionately devoted to what they are doing. Almost any pastor can gain their respect by showing an intelligent, informed, and careful devotion to the same people to whom they also minister daily.

The minister soon learns the drastic limitations on his abilities to help people, even though he is no more limited than other trained workers who are circumscribed in their own particular ways. Then he discovers that it is not so important that he himself help a parishioner as it is that his own personal energies be so strengthened that he can help himself. When he discovers how to lay hold of the resources of all those about him (especially the resources of "those who are of the household of faith") he will be less likely to become "weary in well-doing." And he will find his most loyal friends among those comrades on the "community team."

I. The Ministry of Referral

The minister is responsible, in the presence of a wealth of community resources for helping people, for more than he himself is capable and trained to do for people. He is also obligated to see that they get the help of other professional workers who are equipped to help them with specialized difficulties. It is just as important that a pastor see that a person gets help as it is to give that help himself.

For instance, a pastor in a small county-seat town received a letter from a soldier in occupied Japan. The soldier was distressed over the economic welfare of his wife and children who lived about ten miles out in the country from the town in which the pastor lived and worked. The soldier had tried other avenues of learning about the needs of his wife, who would not write him about the health and economic status of the family. The pastor was much too busy in his own community at the time to give personal attention to the man's request. He knew too that he might not be able to give the assistance needed, even if he should visit the home. Instead of going himself, therefore, he asked a social caseworker in the county welfare department (who was a devoted member of his church) to investigate the matter. She did and, having discovered the needs of the family to be acute, brought the welfare resources of the community to their rescue.

In order that a pastor may take his place with confidence on the " community team " he needs specific guidance on the ministry of referral. He needs to know something of the indications as to *when* he should refer a person to another professional worker. He needs to know some of the methods and the hazards involved in making such referrals. He needs to know the resources of his own community well enough, and should stay in a community long enough to establish a working understanding with other members of the " community team."

A. *The Indications of the Need for Referral*

The pastor needs to ask himself in every situation of pastoral care and personal counseling, " Is this parishioner in need of help other than the specific ministry that I am commissioned and equipped to offer him? " The question may be answered both generally and specifically.

1. *General indications of the need for referral.* (*a*) The minister generally refers a parishioner to others when he knows that more time and attention will be required than he has to offer. For instance, a pastor may even have the necessary training to carry through with deeper-level counseling over a period of weeks and months. Nevertheless, his program at that moment may be so heavy that he cannot

give adequate attention to the person. He may be planning to be out of the community, or he may be so involved in other responsibilities that he cannot possibly find the time necessary to do what needs to be done. Then he will need other trained persons whose time will be available. This may mean that he will refer the individual to an assistant, to another pastor, to a marriage and family counselor, to a psychiatrist, or to a social worker. The person to whom he refers the needy individual will be determined entirely by the kind of problem in need of solution, and the kind of persons available for referral. No specific rule can be devised.

(*b*) Another general consideration on the need for referral is that many ministers can be too socially and emotionally involved with an individual to give the kind of help needed in a given situation. One instance can be cited. A student pastor in a part-time pastorate in the suburbs of a large city sought to counsel with two married couples in his church. All four persons were active members of his church, having places of important leadership. They were contemplating " trading wives and husbands " in a double divorce and remarriage arrangement. Before they did so they brought their confusion to the pastor, who sought to deal with the problem directly, without help. The whole church became involved, and soon the pastor was the target of a cross fire of hostility, which culminated in his resignation from the church. If the pastor had known that the trouble was too involved for him to handle alone, he could have referred the couples to marriage and family counseling agencies in a nearby city. There they would have received expert help, and the church would not have been hurt so deeply as it was.

(*c*) In the third place, the pastor generally refers parishioners whose problems require specialized treatment which the pastor has not been trained to give. This is an easy way of avoiding the responsibility of dealing with the more serious troubles within a congregation. However, even the most highly trained pastors can be identified by their ability to know the limitations of their equipment for dealing with special difficulties.

2. *Specific indications of the need for referral.* (*a*) The parishioner who is physically sick, or who *thinks* that he is physically sick, needs

the help of a good doctor. The pastor should be thoroughly informed
as to the medical help available, both in his community and in the
larger region in which he lives. Especial attention should be given
to the availability of specialized diagnostic and therapeutic services
in medical centers. The cost of such treatment, the various services
of " clinics," and the distances from the person who needs it are practical problems to be confronted. Usually, if a parishioner is already
under the care of a physician, the pastor should by all means confer
with that physician before he takes any important step in counseling
with the person about his or her spiritual difficulties. If the person
does not have a medical doctor at the time, the pastor is at liberty
to suggest the names of doctors with whom he himself has an understanding.

(*b*) The parishioner who is manifestly psychotic needs medical
help. As has already been suggested, these persons quite often come
to the attention of a minister *before* they go to a doctor. If a person
is threatening suicide, if he is dangerous to the personal safety of
other people, if he is not amenable to reason but is deluded and ir-
rational, or if he shows any of the less obvious signs of mental disease, he needs the care of a doctor. If the pastor is acquainted with
the family of the person, he may seek tactfully to instruct the closest
of kin as to the seriousness of the situation. In doing so, the pastor
should avoid " diagnosing " or treating the person's difficulty himself. The extent of his ministry will be directly dependent upon the
co-operation of the family and the availability of psychiatric help.

However, a pastor in a community where there are no psychiatric
facilities and where the general practitioners are extremely old and
poorly trained faces the heavy responsibility of doing for the patient
what he can. He does it " with fear and trembling," taking care to
do no harm. The situation of a pastor in the event that a psychiatrist
is available is much like his relationship to a surgical patient: *Before*
and *during* the illness, his best help is offered in establishing the
confidence of the patient and his family in the doctor's trustworthi-
ness. His ministry *after* the illness is primarily that of helping the
person to find himself in a place of security after his recovery.

(*c*) The unmarried mother needs the help of the minister's wife, the medical resources of the area, and the guidance of a family service organization in addition to the personal ministry of a pastor to her and her family. The maternity homes established by the Salvation Army for unmarried mothers meet an acute need here. The delicacy of the problem and the psychological involvements of most unmarried mothers make it very difficult for a minister to deal with this problem directly. It should be done as indirectly, by way of referral, as is possible without causing the woman to feel rejected by the pastor himself.

(*d*) Another concrete example of the need for referral help is the alcoholic persons with whom every pastor deals. As Dean Sperry has pointed out: "Hitherto ministers have regarded drunkenness as a moral scandal and a vice. They looked to the mourners' bench at a revival meeting as the safest and surest cure. It is only fair to say that this remedy has worked in many classic instances. But today ministers are beginning to realize that there is a point beyond which drunkenness becomes a bodily disease, and the moral resolutions of penitence may well need the fortification of sober medical treatment." [30] Likewise, the reliability of the methods of the Alcoholics Anonymous groups has been demonstrated, and a minister is wise to depend upon these men's help in dealing with acute alcoholism.

(*e*) The poverty-stricken person, in need of economic assistance, is another for whom the pastor usually needs referral help. Much harm has been done to people who were given economic assistance by well-meaning persons who did not know how to get the facts and foundation for wisely doing so. The pastor and his church should be participants in the general welfare program of the community, both in terms of giving support and in terms of referring needy persons to these organizations. The personnel is trained to meet the needs of hungry, naked, and shelterless people. If they are not trained to do so according to wisdom and tenderness, the pastor should be held in enough confidence among the people of the community to be heard when he suggests the need for more adequate workers. The church, of course, will have ways and means of meet-

[30] Willard L. Sperry, *The Ethical Basis of Medical Practice*, p. 23. Paul B. Hoeber, Inc., 1950.

ing the emergency economic needs of its own members. If a dependable family in the community should lose their house and other belongings by fire, the fellowship of the church should be strong enough to keep the family from too much hardship. If a long-term chronic need appears in some family (such as a mother being left a widow with several small children and no relatives to turn to), the pastor may confer with the community service organizations and make a plan whereby a consistent and intelligent program of help can be offered co-operatively. Pastors do well to seek the advice of the welfare agencies as to *how* a family or an individual can be helped without taking away their self-respect and causing them to lose personal initiative.

Many other specific situations can be named in which a pastor needs the help of people to whom he may refer parishioners who come to him for guidance. Young people seeking work may be referred to employers, young persons seeking premarital counseling will be referred to doctors, and those seeking guidance about adoption of children will be referred both to doctors and to social agencies. Parishioners making educational plans will be referred to college and university authorities, and veterans with specific difficulties will be referred to Government agencies that have been established for such purposes.

B. *The Process and the Methods of Referral*

The process of referral and the methods used in carrying through with that process determine to a large extent the amount of good the person gains by the referral.

1. Wittenberg rightly observes that *the first step in the referral is the pastor's own recognition of the problem.*[31] It can be added that the pastor must recognize not only the nature of the parishioner's difficulty but also his own need for help. Naturally, he can overdo this: he can feel so inadequate in the presence of even the most trivial problem that he runs for cover when he sees the first sign of suffering. Or he may simply not want to be bothered at all and

[31] *Op. cit.*, p. 90.

" pass the buck " to someone else. But ordinarily the pastor is over-conscientious instead, and feels that he should have the resources within himself and his knowledge of the Bible to solve any and every problem that arises. In such an instance, the pastor who recognizes his need for help has made a real step in his understanding of himself.

2. *The second step in a referral interview is to interpret the person's own difficulty to him.* A young man comes to his pastor and describes many physical symptoms such as headache, loss of appetite, and sleeplessness. He says, however, that these are all caused by his fears that he is going to " do something " at night to hurt his wife, and by his fear that he is losing his mind. He breaks down, cries profusely, and falls all over the chair, writhing with anxiety. After calming the man, the pastor gets a little more of the story, discovering that the man is hearing strange voices " out of nowhere." Obviously the man needs help, but the pastor recognizes his own inability to minister to him without the help of a good psychiatrist. Therefore, in a persuasive and suggestive manner, the pastor says to him: " You have had these feelings pile up during the rapid events of the past few weeks. You have not been married long; you are facing new responsibilities; you have had several misunderstandings with those who are very close to you; you are afraid of what you think; you are upset, nervous, and have not slept nor eaten properly. I think you realize that you are not in any frame of mind to think through your problems clearly or to make any important decisions at this time, until you have regained your health of body and spirit." This is a common-sense interpretation of his trouble, aimed at suggesting to him the idea that he does not just *think* that he is sick, but that he really *is* sick and needs help in addition to that which the pastor can offer.

3. *The third step in a referral interview is the pastor's confession of his own limitations and the need for the help of the person to whom he hopes to refer the individual.* In the case cited above, the pastor went on to say to him: " Of course, your health is the most important thing to you at this present moment. I can be your friend and talk with you about your relationship to God. I can pray with

you and reassure you of God's love and sustaining power. But your health needs the attention of a doctor, and I know that you cannot be your best spiritual self as long as you are ill in your total make-up. You need to go to a doctor, who can give you treatments that will relax you and restore your perspective, who can talk with you about your ideas and feelings after you have rested awhile. A good psychiatrist can help you with your troubles." Immediately the man said, "But what would my wife think of me?" Then the pastor said, "Well, maybe I could help by talking to your wife also." Fortunately, the pastor found the wife co-operative and he was able to help the patient to accept the fact that he was a sick man and to understand the necessity for psychiatric help.

4. *The fourth step in a referral interview is that in which the pastor gets the parishioner in touch with the person to whom he is referring him.* This is usually done by telephone, but occasionally is done personally. Sometimes, if the situation is not one that involves emergency action, a letter will do. In the case mentioned above, the name, address, and telephone number of the psychiatrist were given to the patient and his wife. The man was admitted to a hospital the next day and received treatment. At this stage, the most important necessity is that the pastor "transfer" whatever confidence the parishioner may have in him as a pastor to the person to whom he is referring him. He will find it necessary to reassure both the patient and the family after this order: "I have known this doctor for some time. I know from observing him that he is trustworthy and deserves your complete confidence. Now that you are in his care, be sure to depend upon him and his guidance without too much fear. He is a good man, and shares the same ideals that you and I share in God." Simple honesty requires that the pastor do his best to find persons about whom he can sincerely say such things.

5. *The fifth phase of such a referral includes co-operative concern and a minimum of interference on the part of the pastor.* One danger in making a referral is that the person referred will feel that the pastor is "trying to get rid of him." In the case under discussion, this was avoided by directly reassuring the patient, by following his progress by telephoning his wife, and by visiting him during his

hospitalization. In referring a patient to a psychiatrist, the pastor does the doctor a great service by writing him a " referral letter " in which he gives a brief summary of the facts which he knows about the patient's situation. This summary should include a word about how this parishioner came to the attention of the pastor, a concise description of the number and nature of conversations the pastor has had with him, a description of his problem in the *same words that he himself used,* in so far as is possible, and a statement of the facts about the life history of the parishioner which the pastor may know.

The summary may be followed by another paragraph in which the pastor gives his own interpretation in *nontechnical language* of the life situation of the person whom he has referred. Such a lengthy letter is indicated in the case of referrals to a doctor, and especially to a psychiatrist, but common sense would counsel against any such approach in simpler difficulties. The case of a psychiatric referral has been cited here because it is the most difficult type of referral that a pastor has to make, and because requests come more often as to how to refer a person to a psychiatrist. Tender persuasion and strong suggestion are necessary in most cases of this kind.

6. *The final phase of a referral is the follow-up.* This corresponds to the phase of follow-up and experimentation characteristic of all good counseling.

A procedure of this kind, skillfully executed, leaves the pastor's hands free for a definitely religious ministry in the life of his people. He can rely upon the resources of his community to help him in such a way that he can do a distinctive task without being a " Jack of all trades and master of none," dabbling in this, that, and the other and not " sticking to his own last " of the reconciliation of men with God. Nevertheless, this does not relieve him of the responsibility of knowing enough about the work of the other members of the " community team " to be able to function smoothly in relation to them.

The question may be properly raised at this point, " What should be done in case a person does not want to co-operate with the referral? " An instance of this is the sixty-five-year-old woman who

constantly sought the help of the church with her financial difficulties. She had no work, wandered about the city begging, would
call the wealthier members of the church by telephone and ask them
for help. If they did not do what she wanted them to do, she would
threaten to kill herself, call them profane names, and become in-
censed with anger. She was the first seeker for help who came to the
attention of every new pastor.

One of the pastors, when she came to him, listened carefully to
her story and asked her to come back to see him the next day. In
the meantime, he called the city relief agencies and discovered that
she had a sixteen-year record with them. She had an epileptic brother
and was considered by the agencies to have "epileptoid personality
traits" herself. They suggested that the pastor refer her to them, and
that the church itself contribute what it could to the total program
of medical and financial relief that the agency would plan for her.

When the woman returned the next day, the pastor, after having
conferred with the social service committee of the church (which
had long since lost patience with her), referred the woman to the
social agency. He said to her: "The church plans to help you if you
will co-operate with us in the program we have outlined for you. I
have talked with the family service organization and asked them
to study your whole financial problem, and I have told them that we
will do for you what they suggest. We will pay our funds directly
to them, and they will add whatever else you need." The woman
became irate and refused to co-operate.

The only thing a pastor can do in a case like this is to be understanding toward such a person, because she is not responsible for
what she does. But there is a limit beyond which a pastor cannot go
in trying to help people. He does them harm when he tries to over-
rule their desire to be helped. Such a procedure will help a pastor to
be objective, and at the same time do all that can be done to meet
people's needs. He is forced to give his time and energy to people
who co-operate.

Anton T. Boisen is fond of saying that the pastor deals with three
groups of people: First, there are those who are capable of taking
care of themselves, and will get along nicely regardless of the care

the pastor gives them. Secondly, there are those who will become progressively worse, regardless of the care and attention the pastor can offer them, and will not profit by anything he does for them because they do not want to be helped. Thirdly, there are those who stand at the crossroads, and the outcome of their lives will be *largely determined* by the patient efforts of a pastor in his ministry to them. Of course, this is a loose but very valuable generalization. The pastor is under obligation to cast his few pearls of time, energy, and equipment where they will do the most good. The parable of the Sower and the Seed and the parable of the Wheat and the Tares can be appreciated best by the veteran pastors who see the magnitude of human suffering and the finitude of their own abilities in the light of the eternal wisdom of God.

APPENDIXES

RESOURCES FOR CLINICAL PASTORAL TRAINING

Pastors and theological students may find a wide variety of training from different points of view in the following organizations. The training falls into two types of organizations: (1) those which conduct their programs independently of, but in co-operation with, theological schools and (2) those which conduct their programs *within* the context of the curriculum of a specific seminary or school of theology.

In the first type of organization may be listed:

THE INSTITUTE OF PASTORAL CARE, under the direction of Rev. Rollin J. Fairbanks. Information concerning the program of six-week seminars in pastoral work may be secured by writing to Mr. Fairbanks at Andover Hall, Cambridge, Massachusetts.

THE COUNCIL FOR CLINICAL TRAINING, INC., under the guidance of Rev. Frederick Kuether, 2 East 103d Street, New York 29, New York. A full catalogue of their activities may be secured by writing to Mr. Kuether. Their programs are twelve weeks in length. In the second type of organization, the following institutions are noteworthy:

ANDOVER NEWTON THEOLOGICAL SCHOOL, under the guidance of Professor Philip Guiles and Professor John Billinsky, Newton Centre, Massachusetts. This work is conducted in co-operation with the Boston City Hospital.

BOSTON UNIVERSITY SCHOOL OF THEOLOGY, under the supervision of Professor Paul E. Johnson.

DUKE DIVINITY SCHOOL, under the supervision of Professor Russell L. Dicks. The Divinity School is next door to Duke Hospital, of which Professor Dicks is chaplain. Full information concerning this program of training may be secured by writing to Professor Russell L. Dicks, Duke Divinity School, University Station, Durham, North Carolina.

DREW THEOLOGICAL SEMINARY, under the direction of Professor Paul B. Maves, Madison, New Jersey.

GARRETT BIBLICAL INSTITUTE, under the guidance of Professor Carroll Wise, Evanston, Illinois.

ILIFF SCHOOL OF THEOLOGY, DENVER, COLORADO, in co-operation with the Denver General Hospital. Professor Dicks has taught summer courses here for several years.

SOUTHERN BAPTIST THEOLOGICAL SEMINARY, under the direction of this author. Full details may be learned concerning both graduate and undergraduate degrees in the field of pastoral care and psychology of religion by writing to Professor Wayne E. Oates, 2825 Lexington Road, Louisville 6, Kentucky. This work is given in co-operation with the Norton Memorial Infirmary Psychiatric Clinic, the Louisville General Hospital, the Central State Hospital (Lakeland, Kentucky), the Kentucky State Hospital (Danville, Kentucky), the Missouri Baptist Hospital (St. Louis, Missouri), and the North Carolina Baptist Hospital (Winston-Salem, North Carolina).

RECORDS OF PASTORAL WORK

Records can become an end within themselves and thereby blight the ministry of a shepherd. But when used as a means of keeping a check on oneself and as a means of pastoral research in themselves, they become a guide to a richer understanding of people. As Washington Gladden has said: "Every minister can be and must be an original investigator. Genuine laboratory work is demanded of him. . . . Firsthand knowledge is imperative."[32] The method whereby he accomplishes this is a carefully recorded analysis of his face-to-face ministry of people.

The working pastor will find that he has need of about four different kinds of records:

I. STATISTICAL RECORDS

Ministers have always felt the necessity of keeping a record of the names, ages, dates, and places of marriages, funerals, and baptisms at which they have officiated. Many ministers also keep a record of their sermon titles, and the places where they have preached these sermons. These records are of great value for reference, and prevent embarrassment when certain occasions arise.

The pastor, however, will profit all the more by keeping a careful record of the following items:

A. Visits he makes to the homes and places of business of his people:
    1. Initial visit.
    2. Follow-up visits.

B. Visits he makes to hospitals and other institutions:
    1. Initial visit.
    2. Follow-up visits.

C. Visits his people make to his home or study, seeking his personal counsel:
    1. Initial visit.
    2. Return visits.

This sort of record may be kept very simply in an anonymous fashion by placing three sheets in the back of a pastoral notebook and tabulating

[32] *Op. cit.,* pp. 93, 94.

them in this fashion. Or a brief card file may be kept, which will include a new entry every time a new person is contacted within the scope of a given year.

The advantage of a record like this is to keep a gauge on the *type* of ministry the pastor is rendering, whether it is one in which people come to him or one in which he must seek them out. Again, the pastor can keep a check on *the relative degree of extensiveness and intensiveness* with which he is functioning with his people. He may be touching a great many people superficially in only one initial interview, or he may be swinging to the other extreme of spending too much time with a relatively few people and neglecting the larger needs of more people.

II. BRIEF PASTORAL NOTES

Another type of record is the sort that identifies the kind of problem the persons present; whether the pastor visits them or is visited by them is of no consequence in this type of record. Here the pastor simply lists the major complaints that experience has taught him:

1. Alcoholism.
2. Bereavement.
3. Divorce.
4. Mental illness:
    a. Psychoneurotics.
    b. Psychotics.
5. Religious doubts and need for conversion.
6. Parent-child conflict.
7. Sexual maladjustment.
8. Vocational decisions.
9. Church-group tensions.

Of course, he may add many others as time goes along; then, he may discover that *all* these thorny symptoms may be present in *one* person who comes to him. His problems in knowing where to list such a person will consist in determining the *dominant,* overruling difficulty that the person is facing.

This type of record can best be kept on a card with a *brief pastoral note* as to the date and the sort of complaint the person presented. If the pastor is in a small church, a confidential notebook with a leaf for each person in the community serves better. In such a case, a " progressive note " sequence can be kept.

III. CONVERSATION SEQUENCE RECORDS

The pastor will occasionally want to keep a record of his ministry to one individual — a record that comes as nearly as possible to recalling *everything that happened in the conversation sequence.* The reasons for this sort of record are manifest: the pastor's work with the person may have been of a controversial nature, and the pastor will want to have a complete record of his dealings with the person. An example of this would be an interview with a young theological student on a controversial point of theology. If there is ever any question, the pastor will not need to tax his memory for the facts. But primarily, the pastor will learn as much about the person as he attempts to recall the sequence of the conversation as he did while he was talking to the person face to face. He will have a means of criticizing his own work with the person. If he does not have a faculty of self-criticism, this may bring one to birth. The pastor can find no more thorough way of self-instruction in the art of pastoral counseling than this.

Abundant examples of this type of history may be found in books by Dr. Russell L. Dicks such as *And Ye Visited Me, The Art of Ministering to the Sick,* and others. Of course, Snyder's *Casebook of Non-directive Counseling* is a phonographically recorded report on such histories. Charles Holman's book *Getting Down to Cases* is of exceptional value also to the pastor. Case histories of this sort are not used by this author for the obvious reasons of personal confidences that have been given by people who are close at hand.

IV. THE REFERRAL HISTORY LETTER

Another practical use of records is in the pastor's referral ministry. Quite often he will refer a person to a doctor, a social agency, or another pastor and need to write that worker a letter concerning the referral. Such a letter should be a succinct, one-or-two-page typewritten letter which includes all the pertinent facts concerning two things: (1) the chronological sequence of life-history events as far as they are known to the pastor. (2) The course of the relationship that the pastor has had to the person.

Again such a letter should carefully keep *facts* separated from *interpretations.* In this way the pastor is first of all a good reporter. He does not editorialize. *After* the facts have been stated, then an interpretative paragraph by the pastor himself becomes very appropriate and in order.

These letters will go in the pastor's confidential file as he continues in his ministry.

V. CONCLUSIONS

A word needs to be said about taking notes during a conference with a person. This writer has found that such a procedure is like using notes in preaching: it gets in the way of the relationship. Likewise, the pastor fails to discipline his attention to recall later the material if it is needed for records.

Furthermore, records of pastoral work, apart from anonymous statistical records, should be kept completely confidential. The pastor should even exercise great care in keeping such material from those who are closely associated with him: secretaries, assistant pastors, education directors, and even members of his own family. However trusted these persons may be, the coloring that confidential information will give them in their attitudes toward persons in the community is unavoidable. Furthermore, unguarded slips of confidence are well nigh impossible to prevent.

A SYSTEMATIC PROGRAM OF STUDY

The following is a selected and descriptive bibliography of books that should be read *in the order in which they are listed* for the maximum benefit. Careful distinction should be drawn between books that a pastor studies himself and those he uses by handing to his people. No good physician hands his patient an anatomy book or a treatise on differential diagnosis!

I. Comprehensive Books on Pastoral Work

These books do not make a specialty of any one phase of pastoral work such as pulpit work, visiting the sick or counseling with people who have deep-seated emotional conflicts. They are of a general nature, but nevertheless are very valuable in helping a pastor to gain and maintain *a total perspective of his complete function as a minister.*

1. Washington Gladden, *The Christian Pastor and the Working Church.* Charles Scribner's Sons, 1898. 485 pages. This is an old book, but nevertheless of inestimable value for the profundity of Christian experience with which it is written. Then, too, certain passages in it are as contemporary as one's next breath.

2. Andrew W. Blackwood, *Pastoral Work; A Source Book for Ministers.* The Westminster Press, 1945. 252 pages. This book is comprehensive and offers many specific suggestions to pastors. It will be of special use to men who are planning their "first pastorate" relationships and practices. This book has the advantage of the veteran experience of its author.

3. Russell L. Dicks, *Pastoral Work and Personal Counseling,* Revised Edition. The Macmillan Company, 1949. xii, 195 pages.

Professor Dicks's book has combined the current popular interest in personal counseling with the comprehensive approach of Gladden and Blackwood. He shows firsthand acquaintance with what has been done recently in related fields, such as in the work of Carl Rogers. This makes good transitional reading to the next type of literature.

II. SPECIALIZED BOOKS ON PASTORAL COUNSELING

1. J. S. Bonnell, *Psychology for Pastor and People*. Harper & Brothers, publishers, 1948. xii, 225 pages.

This is probably the most popular book in the field of specialized reading on pastoral counseling. The main strength of the book lies in the forthrightness of the author's spiritual convictions. The main weakness lies in the fact that the author assumes that *every* pastor is in a situation similar to his own: a large, metropolitan church with a " clinic " approach to pastoral work, free to use " office techniques." This is true of only a small number of ministers; for the others the book may be misleading. Again, the author of this book assumes that his readers have the same amount of experience in recognizing mental symptoms that he himself has from having spent his life working with mentally disturbed people. This is a rash assumption, and the direct techniques he suggests could do damage if used by a novice.

2. Rollo May, *The Art of Counseling; How to Gain and Give Mental Health*. Abingdon-Cokesbury Press, 1939. 247 pages.

This book lays a sound emphasis upon the importance of the personality of the minister himself in counseling with others, upon the structure and function of personality, and upon the necessity for " empathy " in " feeling one's way into " the very atmosphere of a parishioner's life situation. The book is weighted so heavily with psychoanalytic defenses and jargon that it may produce confusion in the mind of a person who has nothing more than hearsay about the Freudian school of thought and practice. Some excellent principles are set forth, but the reader finishes the book without feeling that he has any specific suggestions as to techniques of counseling.

3. Seward Hiltner, *Pastoral Counseling*. Abingdon-Cokesbury Press, 1949. 291 pages.

The author of this book has been connected with the clinical training movement for many years. He has an encyclopedic knowledge and cosmopolitan experience with the books and authors in the field of pastoral counseling as well as with those in allied fields of clinical psychology, psychiatry, and psychoanalysis. This book therefore is not light reading, nor will the average pastor find it very relevant to the issues which he himself faces. But the student who is making a specialty of this phase of work will find the book invaluable as a guide in traversing the whole field. For instance, this writer has found the book very useful in dealing with graduate students, but little less than confusing to undergraduate students in the field.

4. Rudolph Wittenberg, *So You Want to Help People; A Mental*

Hygiene Primer for Group Leaders. Association Press, 1948. xv, 174 pages.

Most of a minister's work is done with groups, and his counseling is quite often most advantageously done in groups. This book gives a simple but thoroughly dependable description of the dynamics of group behavior and the principles of group counseling. This is an invaluable addition to the pastor's perspective of his total task.

5. A. T. Boisen, *The Exploration of the Inner World; A Study of Mental Disorder and Religious Experience.* Willett, Clark & Company, 1936. xii, 322 pages.

This book, written by the founder of the movement for the specialized training of ministers in the care of the mentally ill, is "strong meat," intended for mature minds and not for novices or babes in Christian thought and experience. The theological significance of the inner problems of psychotic people is dealt with at length here, without at the same time sacrificing firsthand reference to clinical histories. The reader at first will be disturbed by the contents of this book, but he will find himself going back again and again to ponder over the contents. The more experience he has with people in living situations, the more valuable the book will become to him.

6. Richard Cabot and Russell L. Dicks, *The Art of Ministering to the Sick.* The Macmillan Company, 1936. vi, 384 pages.

A medical doctor and a minister-chaplain have combined their insight and experience in writing this book about the ministry to physically ill people. In addition to being good instruction for the minister in his work with sick people, this book compares with Boisen's book favorably in that it too is a masterpiece of beauty in style and diction. Just as the care of the mentally ill by ministers has been centered around Boisen's work, also more serious attention to the problems of the physically ill has been provoked by the work of Professor Dicks. This book, although invaluable, stands in need of revision that will bring it up to date.

III. BOOKS OF VALUE FROM ALLIED FIELDS OF SERVICE AND RESEARCH

A. *Marriage and Family Counseling*

1. Ernest R. and Catherine Groves, *Dynamic Mental Hygiene, with Special Emphasis on Family Counseling.* Stackpole & Heck, Inc., 1946. 559 pages.

If a pastor is going to buy one comprehensive work in this field, this book more nearly meets the need. It is an encyclopedic volume with a wealth of dependable research on every page.

2. Sidney E. Goldstein, *Marriage and Family Counseling; A Manual for Ministers, Doctors, Lawyers, Teachers, Social Workers, and Others*

Engaged in Counseling Service. McGraw-Hill Book Company, Inc., 1945. xvi, 457 pages.

The author of this book has given the marriage and family counselor specific suggestions as to the "how" of both premarital and marital counseling. The routine questions that need to be asked and the specific suggestions that need to be made are discussed at length in these pages.

3. Ernest R. Groves, *Christianity and the Family.* The Macmillan Company, 1942. viii, 229 pages.

Ministers in particular are the audience for whom this book was written by one of the leading sociologists of this century. Groves shows sympathetic appreciation for the Christian faith, and keen understanding of the pastoral relationship.

B. *Clinical Psychology*

1. Carl R. Rogers, *Counseling and Psychotherapy; Newer Concepts in Practice.* Houghton Mifflin Company, 1942. 450 pages.

This book is a basic technical volume. Its strength lies in the use of actual phonographic recordings of interviews as illustrative material, and in the complete history of a counseling relationship with one "Herbert Bryan" as a concluding section of the book. Manifestly the minister cannot take all that Rogers says at face value and make an identical carry over of methods in his work. The minister must be more realistic than Rogers and accept frankly the fact that he does have certain broad objectives that he is seeking to accomplish. This would be the main criticism of this book: the author works consistently toward the objectives of health, emotional maturity, and self-acceptance through personal insight, yet he says the counselor should not think of himself as one who is "assisting in the solution of problems" (p. 28). Nevertheless, this book cannot be dispensed with, and must be given careful consideration if one is to be literate at all in the more serious aspects of personal counseling.

(See also Rogers' latest book, *Client-centered Therapy.*)

2. William U. Snyder, *et al., Casebook of Non-directive Counseling.* Houghton Mifflin Company, 1948. 339 pages.

Five cases are reported in this volume as further illustrations of the Rogers method of nondirective counseling. The minister will find these to be useful in following the "process of counseling" described in this present volume.

C. *Psychiatry*

1. Karl Menninger, *The Human Mind,* Third Edition. Alfred A. Knopf, 1947. 517 pages.

This book takes the plain facts of the field of psychiatry and states them in understandable language. The minister will find that the section on the application of psychiatry to religion is of inestimable value, both in its cautions and its challenge. This book also has vital significance for the preaching message of the minister as he tries to set forth the Christian faith as " the religion of a sound mind." Likewise, the author's other books, *Man Against Himself* and *Love Against Hate,* have inspirational as well as educational value.

2. D. K. Henderson and R. D. Gillespie, *A Text-Book of Psychiatry for Students and Practitioners,* Fourth Edition. Oxford University Press, 1944. 719 pages.

This book is the classical volume used in most medical schools in teaching psychiatry. It describes the syndromes of mental illnesses, the representative therapies, and the possible prognoses of the many different types of disorders.

3. Helen Flanders Dunbar, *Mind and Body: Psychosomatic Medicine.* Random House, Inc., 1947. ix, 263 pages.

This is a simply and beautifully written volume by the outstanding authority on the relation between emotions and bodily changes. The minister owes it to his own edification in the awesome mystery of the human psyche and soma to lay hold of this book.

D. *Psychoanalysis*

1. Sigmund Freud, *A General Introduction to Psychoanalysis.* The Garden City Publishing House Co., Inc., 1920. 410 pages.

Whereas a minister will not agree with all that Freud had to say about any one problem, he will profit by the scientific discoveries the man made with reference to the structure and function of the " natural man." It is as Gregory Zilboorg says: " Before long Freud discovered that he was describing the condition of a man in a state of sin." One reason that ministers are so ineffective at times in dealing with people in " bondage to sin " is that they do not understand their plight. This book, if read with an open mind, will give a minister two things: an accurate description of " the natural man " of which Paul speaks, and, second, a factual basis for criticizing what Freud said and did.

2. Theodor Reik, *Listening with the Third Ear; The Inner Experience of a Psychoanalyst.* Farrar, Straus and Company, Inc., 1948. 514 pages.

The author gives a thorough description of the therapeutic process followed in his own clinical practice. It is autobiographical in nature, and will give a profound insight into the struggle that the psychoanalyst puts up in his own mind with his own tendencies to become the " god " of the patient. The grasp that the author has upon the study of literature and language, the poetic prose in which he writes, and the use he makes of his own experiences make this book valuable from many different points of view.

3. Otto Rank, *Will Therapy, and Truth and Reality*. Alfred A. Knopf, 1945. 291 pages.

This author was connected with the psychoanalytic movement and broke away from it. His criticisms of Freud are the most effective ones from the point of view of a Christian minister. This book is written in simple language, but its content is heavy and the book cannot be read quickly. The theological issues of human experience are frankly confronted, and the man who wrote it will be judged to be " not far from the kingdom." He speaks of the therapeutic situation as being a " birth process," and the " birth of creativity." Rollo May leans very heavily upon the insights of this author in his popular book *Springs of Creative Living*.

4. Karen Horney, *Our Inner Conflicts: A Constructive Theory of Neurosis*. W. W. Norton & Company, Inc., 1946. 250 pages.

The minister who reads this book will find that the author is most friendly to the value of religion and morality, giving an ethical interpretation of the plight of the neurotic. Horney depends much upon the wisdom of the Danish theologian Sören Kierkegaard in this volume, and shows a personal acquaintance with the Greek language in her description of the movements of the emotions of the neurotic.

E. *Books of Value from the Field of Realistic Literature*

1. Nathaniel Hawthorne, *The Scarlet Letter*.

A forceful reminder of the power of the group to heal or hurt, the weight of an unconfessed sin, and the laws of retribution in human affairs. No minister should begin his work as a pastor without having read this precious bit of literary perfection which can be bought very inexpensively at the nearest drugstore. If a pastor has not read it, he should go no further until he has.

2. William Shakespeare, *Hamlet*. The greatest English writer of all times describes in his own unique way a man who could not make up his own mind. The pastor will return to this play perennially.

3. Fëdor Dostoevski, *The Brothers Karamazov*.

The inner workings of the human heart and the clash of emotions within a family are laid bare here. The wistful, yearning quest of the soul of men after the Christ finds its expression here, too.

THE PASTOR'S LOAN SHELF

Every pastor can employ small, readable, and inexpensive books in the pastoral care and personal counseling of individuals and groups. A careful distinction should be made between books that the pastor studies for his own instruction, as those listed in the preceding pages, and the books that he uses as " pastoral aids " in the instruction of persons with whom he counsels. A pastor should have read a book himself before he hands it to another person as help on a specific problem. He should not hand a heavy, lengthy, and expensive volume to another person for therapeutic help. It should be more popularly written, brief, and easily replaced at a minimum cost.

The Westminster Press has begun a series of books that meet these specifications. They are called " The Westminster Pastoral Aid Books." " In contrast to many works written for the use of the pastor alone, containing instructions on procedure and policy in counseling, these books may be placed in the hands of laymen, to speak for the pastor and work for him in aiding persons with physical, mental, and spiritual sufferings " (from the flyleaves of the volumes).

Two of these books have been published thus far:

Russell L. Dicks, *My Faith Looks Up.* A book for the physically ill.

William F. Rogers, *Ye Shall Be Comforted.* A book for the bereaved.

A list of other books that meet these purposes is as follows:

Gordon W. Allport, *The Individual and His Religion; A Psychological Interpretation.* The Macmillan Company, 1950. Well-educated persons who are having serious religious doubts will find positive guidance in this book.

Frederick W. Brink, *This Man and This Woman; A Guide for Those Contemplating Marriage.* Association Press, 1948. A good, all-round volume to hand to couples who are preparing for marriage.

Ernest R. Groves, *Conserving Marriage and the Family.* The Macmillan Company, 1944. Helpful to couples who are having marital conflicts, and especially if they are contemplating divorce.

Charles T. Holman, *Psychology and Religion for Everyday Living.* The Macmillan Company, 1949. Valuable for persons who feel themselves to be " psychological problems."

William Osler, *Way of Life.* Paul B. Hoeber, Inc., 1937. Especially helpful to apprehensive, anxious persons who fear the future.

William Lyon Phelps, *Marriage.* E. P. Dutton & Co., Inc., 1941. A literary masterpiece. An essay that gives both guidance and inspiration to a married couple, and sets a poetic tone for an engaged couple's hopes.

George H. Preston, *The Substance of Mental Health.* Farrar & Rinehart, Inc., 1943. A plain statement of the development of a healthy mind and useful personality. Written in nontechnical language for lay persons.

Douglas V. Steere, *Doors Into Life; Through Five Devotional Classics.* Harper & Brothers, publishers, 1948. An introduction to the great devotional classics. Helpful in guiding college students in a mature practice of personal worship.

James Stewart, *The Strong Name*. Charles Scribner's Sons, 1941. A homiletical approach to the problems of the meaning of suffering. Useful to the person who takes his theology and his Bible seriously.

INDEX

INDEX

Alcoholism, 144
Allport, G. W., 17
Ambivalence, 112, 129
Appointments and their uses, 79, 82 f.,
116, 117 f.

Bereavement, 21 ff., 97
Bibliographical helps, 23 ff., 159 ff.
Birth, psychological significance of,
15
Boisen, Anton T., 149
Bonnell, J. S., 92, 102
Bonthius, R. H., 130

Catharsis, 99
Cedarleaf, J. L., 62
Church administration, philosophy of,
73 f.
Church, the, 40 ff.; and older people,
62; and the need for community,
71 ff.; and the sense of sin and
guilt, 71; and healing, 20 f., 72; as
a social setting for counseling, 83 ff.
Clinical pastoral training, 14, 89, 115,
153 f.
Conscience, 28
Confession, 22, 38, 102 ff.
Conversion, 16 ff., 44 ff., 71 f.
Counseling, conditioning factors in,
77 ff.; dialectical, 110 f.; and fear,
35; group counseling, 16, 19, 40 f.,
68; marriage and family counseling, 19, 62, 98; passivity and over-
dependence in, 123, 126, 135; process of, 116 ff.; reassurance in, 99;
records of, 155; referral in, 65, 84,
86, 89, 141 ff.; resistance in, 122;

relaxation in, 101 f., 121; repression
in, 53 f., 129; self-acceptance in,
130; sin and guilt in, 102 ff.; suggestion in, 98; teaching in, 107 ff.;
theological context of, 26, 77 ff.,
113 ff.; time element in, 39, 65,
81 ff., 142; in vocational choice,
18 ff.
Crises, 13 ff., 97
Cultural pattern, 87 ff.

Davis, Clifford E., 54
Death, 22
Dialectical pastoral care and personal
counseling, 110 f.
Dicks, Russell L., 33, 114, 128
Divorce, 23, 47 f.
Dying persons, the pastoral care of,
22, 97

Edwards, R. H., 33

Fear in the counseling relationship,
35
Freud, Sigmund, 53 f., 122

Gladden, Washington, 21, 56, 104 f.
Grief, the psychological process of, 21
Group counseling, 16, 19, 40 f., 68,
108 f.

Health, physical and mental, 88 ff.
Hawthorne, Nathaniel, 113
Hodges, O. J., 70
Horney, Karen, 115
Holy Spirit, the work of the, 36 ff.